TIME MANAGEMENT FOR CLAIMS PROFESSIONALS

KEVIN M. QUINLEY, CPCU

The
NATIONAL
UNDERWRITER
Company

The National Underwriter Co. • PO Box14367 • Cincinnati, OH 45250-0367
1-800-543-0874 • www.nuco.com

Contents

Chapter One

INTRODUCTION:

Time Management Myths And Realities

"Dammit, Jones, why can't you do something as simple as report a case? You have twelve late statuses!"

"Hey man, when you gonna' come see my car? It's been sittin' here all day! I wanna' talk to your supervisor!"

"Honestly, Dave, sometimes I think you're married to your job and not to me. You spend all your time at the office and the family never sees you. This adjusting work is killing us!"

"This is Willy — when the $%^& are you gonna' send me my check?!?!"

Stomachs churn, blood pressures rise and palms sweat as deadlines mount. Insurance claim professionals feel besieged and experience intense time pressures. "Air traffic controllers never have a nice day," say the guardians of the nation's skies. Claim professionals everywhere relate to the sentiment. The push to do more in less time is not unique to the loss adjustment industry. Time is a finite resource, while the number of assignments is theoretically unlimited. Could the antacid industry survive without the claims profession?

Let's examine one barely fictionalized example:

> Donna has been a claim supervisor for almost a year, and often wonders why she ever wanted the job. Being responsible for five property adjusters, she never has enough time. Between reading files, answering complaints, fielding phone calls, appraising performances and making case assignments, she always feels

behind. "I long for the days when all I had to be concerned with was my own cases..." she states.

Adjusters suffer from poverty; not a financial poverty, but rather a poverty of time. There is an abundance (an embarrassment of riches?) when it comes to claim files. There is a shortage of hours in the day. Americans are finding themselves spending more and more time each year on the job. In fact, a recent study performed by the Economic Policy Institute found that during the past two decades, Americans have increased by 158 hours a year the amount of time they spend at work (*Washington Post,* July 17, 1994, p. A15, "Busy People Hiring Entrepreneurs to Do Their Chores"). This is almost an extra month of work each year.

While this time poverty cuts across vocational boundaries, there is little doubt that work continues to encroach upon the schedules of busy adjusters, testing their time management skills to the max. Productivity (or lack thereof) is the largest single challenge confronting the insurance claims industry today — not bad faith, lack of computers or a dearth of MBA's. Adjusters manufacture nothing. All they have to give is their time. Many problems — lack of thorough investigation, poor customer service, bad faith short-cuts — have as their common root a poverty of time.

The claim profession has at times suffered from a generation gap. Old timers wax nostalgic about the "good old days" when every claim involved face-to-face contact. "What's wrong with the new corps of claim adjusters?" is the oft-heard lament. My first two bosses, veteran claim managers who learned the business in the 1940's and 1950's, often ventilated these views. Typical of this type of reminiscence are statements such as, "In the 1960's, claims handling by insurance companies was a hands-on operation." And, "... in the 50's, most claim departments had veteran experienced adjusters. . ."[1] Is this nostalgia for bygone days, or simple dementia over a past which never really existed?

The supposed demise in today's adjusting skills has been attributed to just about everything: inadequate public education, the spread of telephone communications, society's obsession with instant gratification, even the entry of "yuppies" and women into the insurance work force. The problem has been attributed to just about everything but the most obvious cause: increasing adjuster

2

caseloads per person, leaving less time per claim. Sometimes we overlook the most obvious factors staring us in the face.

SELECTIVE MEMORIES?

Is this senility or just plain forgetfulness? Glossed over is the fact that this golden era preceded the advent of telephone adjusting or recorded statements. Caseloads per adjuster were more likely 30 instead of 250. The Claim Department Manual of Procedures was probably a notebook instead of a three-volume opus. Yesterday's claim professional may have serviced losses for a half-dozen clients instead of 50, each of whom has a different procedural wrinkle. Modern adjusters must run a mine-field, adhering to Unfair Claim Practice Acts, the latest pronouncements handed down from the empyrean reaches of the Home Office, or the latest legal wrinkle in extra-contractual liability ... or bad faith. Each new law or court decision dictates changes in procedures, company policies, paperwork — in short, a new drain on adjuster time.

Adjusters do not work in a vacuum, and the external economy and financial environment impacts their time. Insurance cycles pressure claim operations to trim costs: leaner staffs, increased caseloads per person, enlarged areas of job responsibility. When economizing pressures build, the Claims Department is a prime target. As one observer notes, trying to reduce claim costs by trimming staffs is like trying to fight crime by reducing the police force![2] Without exploring the folly this invites, adjusting staffs will probably remain vulnerable to such shortsightedness. Claim professionals beware: things will get busier. ("Caveat adjustor," as remarked the ancient Roman jurist Octavius Flatus Precipitous in the case of Ben Hur v. Gluteus Maximus, a landmark claim involving a two-chariot intersection collision and indigestible fig leaves.)

Even in healthy financial times for the whole industry, the claims person is not likely to see a slackening workload. Society is becoming increasingly litigious. Courts and legislatures devise new theories of recovery and expand novel coverage interpretations. More claims are spawned at a time when companies seek to trim loss adjustment staffs. Law schools continue to disgorge increasing numbers of newly-minted attorneys.

Demographic trends signal a crying need for time management skills as well. More women are entering the claims profession. As

3

they juggle the new demands of career and personal life, women will feel unprecedented demands on their time. Sheer growth of population, and of the number of lawyers in particular, increases the likelihood that claim volume will grow unabated.

Today's consumer (and claimant) tends to be much more demanding than yesterday's, and this exerts further pressure on an adjuster's time. Consumerism runs rampant; this is not necessarily bad. One byproduct of today's consumerism is that people want it done *yesterday!* They demand their rights! They know someone who read somewhere that in California there was a guy with the same injury who got TEN MILLION DOLLARS! In fact, Uncle Hugo bought his yacht from the proceeds of an insurance settlement he got for his sciatica and whiplash following a low-speed collision. So they complain, push and are intolerant of what they perceive to be delays. This sets a high standard of expectations. Insurers need to provide prompt service. The flip side of the coin, though, is that time pressures on claims professionals — those foot soldiers of insurance service — are increasing, heightening the need for time management skills.

ALL LEVELS AFFECTED

Paperless files and offices remain lofty goals, largely unattained in today's claim operations, unless you happen to work in San Antonio, Texas, where USAA has come closer to this ideal than perhaps anyone. Despite trends toward automation and computerization, the claims business remains labor- and paper-intensive. Computers cannot (yet!) take statements or conduct activity checks. Mounds of paperwork remain the rule, not the exception in loss adjusting. The problem is not confined to field-level employees, but extends into middle and upper management.

> A 1980 study by the Booz Allen & Hamilton management consulting firm found... that business managers often spend no more than 29% of their time on actual "thought work" such as reading, creating documents and problem-solving. More often, the workday gets drained away in such time-consuming and distracting activities as arranging meetings and conferences, searching for information and waiting for the preparation and delivery of reports and studies.[3]

Computerization and office automation have hardly lightened management's load. Paper consumption has actually increased since the advent of office computers. Now, we have more memos, spreadsheets, printouts and reports to read than ever. We suffer from information overload at a time when we seem to have less time than ever before. In a survey conducted by global recruiter Robert Half International, vice-presidents and personnel directors of America's 100 largest companies were asked what time they got up in the morning. The average time was 5:49 a.m. Thirty two percent reported they rise no later than 5:30 a.m. How about arrival time at work? They average arrival time was 7:35 a.m. Sixteen percent said they get to the office by 7:00 a.m.[4] Somehow the wonders of office automation haven't seemed to trickle up to the management level, or has created more work through around-the-clock accessibility.

Once you climb the organizational pecking order, your time management skills are only tested more.

"I thought time problems were over once you got to be a manager" remarked Gordon, claims manager for a large commercial lines carrier. "Boy, was I wrong! The demands on my time have easily tripled. Refereeing staff disputes, keeping on top of reports my Home Office requires, and putting out fires takes up most of all my time. When am I supposed to have time for planning, marketing calls or preparing a budget?"

In one sense, everyone with whom the claims professional deals is a "claimant," in that they lay claim to the adjuster's time. Claims people must walk a thin line with regard to their time. On the one hand, they need uninterrupted periods in which to accomplish the necessary jobs of investigating, negotiating, evaluating, etc. On the other hand, they must be accessible to simultaneously report to various constituencies. Reporting time usurps energies which could be channelled into actually doing.

MANY BALLS TO JUGGLE

Adjusters do not have the luxury of simply adjusting claims. In fact, the plethora of ancillary demands may even leave them with less and less time to actually handle claims. Claims people do not enjoy many periods of uninterrupted concentration. They must simultaneously *do* claims work and provide a running commentary on what they are doing to: insureds, interested claimants, clients, lawyers, physicians, bosses and Home Offices. Time spent reporting to these multiple constituencies drains energy which could be spent actually working cases. This constraint further bogs down efforts, producing delays and yet further "inquiries" to claims professionals about what they are doing. In this context lies much of the claims person's time dilemma.

This may sound natural and not so daunting. Imagine, however, a heart surgeon who is not only expected to perform delicate surgery but who, during the operation, must also simultaneously answer questions from the gallery about what he has done, why he has done it, when he will be finished and why he hasn't attended to the seven other patients who are waiting for him. This is the claim person's plight.

Are we having fun yet?

NO SEX APPEAL

Time management suffers from either a "bum rap" or being mislabeled as a yuppie topic. The phrase evokes images of beady-eyed behavioral scientists with stopwatches and pocket protectors, a kind of "Revenge of the Nerds" sequel. In the TV series L.A. Law, the partners at the fictitious firm of McKenzie Brachman spurned a lucrative merger with a larger firm when the latter arrives with a team of efficiency consultants. This is an unfortunate and undeserved stereotype. The idea that efficiency is dehumanizing is often used to rationalize time mismanagement. Time management ranks right up there with Federal Reserve Board proceedings on the "ho-hum" scale. Time management often makes people uneasy.

Many misconceptions surround the topic of time management. Let's examine some of the most prominent:

Myth #1: "It's foolish to try to manage time because no one work day is like the other." Adjusters do enjoy a variety of work situations from day to day (if "enjoy" is the right word). While no one day is exactly like another, certain common denominators can likely be found in each claim person's work day: answering phones, handling paper flow, attending meetings, taking statements, negotiating claims, etc. You do not have to do the same thing each day, i.e. tighten a widget, in order to work more efficiently using sound time management principles. Time management is not just for folks with cookie-cutter, assembly-line jobs.

Myth #2: "Time management can't work in a claims setting because there are too many unforeseeables." Are they are unforeseeable or merely unforseen? There is a big difference. Dominance of the unexpected may be a symptom of the need for time management. Many crises plaguing claim departments are recurring. If the sources of crises are diagnosed and the responses anticipated, perhaps claim departments would spend less time putting out fires. The presence of "unforeseeables" argues even more compellingly for the need for time management. Establishing protocols for handling crises makes them more manageable.

Myth #3: "The claims business is people-intensive and time management is not a good idea." While it is true that the claims field is people- and not capital-intensive, this is one more good reason to intelligently manage time. Time management does not require ignoring co-workers, your staff or your boss. On the contrary, it includes consciously scheduling more time for each. To the extent that your time is used more efficiently, you will likely have more time for people and people-problems.

Myth #4: "Claims people are too busy to plan their time." If they're too busy, that's all the more reason to plan.
Minutes spent planning save hours in execution.
He who fails to plan, plans to fail.
Claims people too busy to plan may not remain employed in the business very long. One observer notes, "It's a vicious cycle, because the less time we have, the less we plan, and the less we plan, the more time it takes to do the job - so we run out of time."[5] Claims people are very busy and are likely to get busier. These time demands argue even more persuasively for the need to plan one's time.

Myth #5: "The real way to get ahead in the claims field is to work harder." Who can argue against the Puritan work ethic? The answer, though, may lie in working smarter, not harder. Or in working smarter *and* harder. They are not mutually exclusive. At one extreme is the philosophy proclaimed by one wit: "Hard work never hurt, but why take the chance?" At the other, more preferred end of the spectrum is the combining of hard work and efficiency. Consultant Marilyn Machlowitz observes that:

> More than one workaholic has worked very hard on the wrong things. Believing in the adage, "When in doubt, work", they just work harder.[6]

By working harder, longer and more efficiently, businessman and race-car owner Roger Penske has an "unfair advantage" over his competitors, according to one profile of the race-car magnate.

There is a parable of a woodcutter who became increasingly inefficient at chopping down trees, because his axe had become dull. Pretty soon, it took him twice as long to chop down the same number of trees. A friend asked him why he simply didn't get his axe blade sharpened. "I'm too busy chopping down these trees!" was the retort.

Time management is a way for you to sharpen your axe. Claims people can get more done in less time, magnifying their effectiveness and thereby enhancing their promotability. In the process, claim people adept at managing their time will find they have more time for life outside their jobs. Moral: Use this book to sharpen *your* axe!

Myth #6: "Time management is an interesting topic I'll explore when I become a [Supervisor/Examiner/Manager]. It doesn't relate to my job as an adjuster." Procrastination raises its ugly head here: "I think I'll start my diet/exercise programs/study tomorrow." Truth is, adjusting work offers a gold mine of opportunity for intelligent time management. By applying time management principles discussed here, adjusters will have a competitive edge in getting that Supervisor/Examiner/Manager job much more quickly. Time management is not something to be considered only by the upper echelon of the claims hierarchy.

It is true that one cannot literally "save" time. Time is a fixed-supply commodity. We cannot manufacture more. We each have a limited amount, even though we don't know exactly how much.

Real estate tycoons advocate investing in land because, "they aren't making any more." The same can be said of time, and it is an equally stellar investment. While it is not possible to save up time as one would save coins in a piggy bank, one can waste time. It is also possible to use one's time in a way that helps you achieve what you want in life — your personal and professional life.

Inefficiency through time waste exacts a staggering financial toll on American businesses. Robert Half states that time lost within American organizations constitutes a yearly monetary loss of $100 billion.[7] While no separate studies have been conducted on time waste in the insurance field, observation supports the view that there is room for improvement. Claim professionals can apply time management and techniques and concepts to their jobs. They can get more done in less time, and still be human. Becoming an efficient robot is not necessary. Time management can make your personal and professional life more rewarding. Managing time is a life skill, applicable to activities away from the job. Conversely, inability to manage time is a life problem.

Insurance is a service industry based on information, not on manufacturing. In his book, *Megatrends,* author John Naisbitt foresees the economy becoming increasingly based on service and information sectors. Given the demographics of this trend, it is likely that demands upon the time of claim professionals will greatly increase, making the ability to manage time more valuable for those pursuing insurance careers.

NOT FOR ADJUSTERS ONLY

Any insurance professional can benefit from this book, though claims professionals will find much here from which they can particularly profit and to which they can relate. For very definite reasons, this work is not titled "Time Management for Insurance Adjusters." **The ideas developed here are useful to all claim professionals across the job spectrum.** Intelligent time use is not a skill that adjusters alone can enjoy, but they are prime candidates in needing to be proficient at it. Others within the claims profession — claim technicians, supervisors, examiners, claim managers and executives — can use the same techniques.

Shelves groan under the weight of time management literature. Books and articles about technical aspects of claims-handling also

9

abound. Books and tapes on the science of negotiation have produced a mini-industry. Such references are undoubtedly essential to learning the ropes. A synthesis of this material is lacking, however. Textbooks and reference sources on claims dodge or ignore the unique time management needs and demands of claim professionals.

Ivory Towerism often prevents critics from seriously examining the time management problem of today's claim professionals. Books and articles focus on variations of technical themes: "How to Investigate Better," "How to Negotiate," or "Avoiding Bad Faith." Some commentators write as though each claims person had limitless amounts of time to spend on a caseload of four files, as they pine for a return to back-to-basics adjusting. Trade press columnists lamenting the current level of adjusting skill often overlook the obvious problem: with rising caseloads, adjusters lack the skills to manage their time. Nor are they even taught such skills.

Claim training programs often assume that adjusters know all they need to know about managing time and that they merely need to memorize provisions from the Personal Automobile Policy or recite verbatim the law-book definition of "tort." Courses on management and MBA programs frequently neglect time management. Mark McCormack included personal time management among those subjects that they DON'T teach you at Harvard Business School. They don't teach it much at adjusting schools, either. There is a huge need for a knowledge of time management techniques on the part of today's adjusting corps.

Offered here is an application of time-tested techniques to the job of a busy claim professional. For those interested in exploring the topic further, an annotated bibliography for further reading is supplied. These tips have been distilled from almost two decades of experience in the claim field, interviews with claims professionals and a long-standing fascination with the subject of how to work smarter, not necessarily harder. The author hopes this book will be a user-friendly desk-side reference for claim professionals who want to use their time more intelligently, but who don't want work to overshadow their entire life.

In other words, you don't have to be a nerd to manage your time well!

NOTES

1. "Big Loss Ratios: The High Price of Weaker Claims Efforts," *National Underwriter.* August 10, 1987, p.23.

2. Ibid. p. 34.

3. "Fighting the Paper Chase," *Time.* January 23, 1981, p.66.

4. "Corporate Execs Up and At 'Em," *National Underwriter.* August 1, 1986, p. 41.

5. Martin M. Broadwell and William F. Simpson, *The New Insurance Supervisor.* Reading, Mass. Addison-Wesley, 1981, p. 163.

6. Marilyn Machlowitz, *Workaholics: Living With Them, Working With Them.* Reading Mass. Addison-Wesley, 1980, p. 50.

7. Lauren R. Januz and Susan K. Jones, *Time Management for Executives.* New York: Charles Scribner's Sons, 1981, p. 103.

Chapter Two

Taking Your "Time Management Temperature"

Start managing your time well by self-appraising your current habits. Take the following quiz to help determine your own needs for improved time management. Due to conflicting job duties, there are two separate appraisals: two different check-ups for those claim professional with and without management/supervisory responsibilities. Obviously there will be some overlap, since some time management skills are critical regardless of whether or not one supervises, manages or is simply responsible for one's own caseload. While there are no right or wrong answers, the higher the score, the more you need this book:

ADJUSTER APPRAISAL	YES	USUALLY	SOME	RARELY	NEVER
I keep a specific written list of career goals.	1	2	3	4	5
I have recorded my time use within the past year.	1	2	3	4	5
I have written objectives and priorities each day.	1	2	3	4	5
I keep all my cases on a diary system.	1	2	3	4	5
I rank daily priorities, starting with the most important.	1	2	3	4	5

	YES	USUALLY	SOME	RARELY	NEVER
Each day I schedule blocks of un-interrupted time.	1	2	3	4	5
I have eliminated recurring crises.	1	2	3	4	5
I finish one task before starting another one.	1	2	3	4	5
I plan my time on a weekly and monthly basis.	1	2	3	4	5
I work my cases and do not let them "work me."	1	2	3	4	5
I am pro-active as opposed to re-active with my claims.	1	2	3	4	5
I put travel and waiting time to good use.	1	2	3	4	5
I keep reference materials and forms stocked at my desk.	1	2	3	4	5
I am prepared for the unexpected regarding on-the-scene investigations.	1	2	3	4	5
I work with the receptionist/secretary to help me manage in-coming phone calls.	1	2	3	4	5
I put telephone time "on hold" to good use.	1	2	3	4	5
I take time each day to do nothing.	1	2	3	4	5
I have little trouble getting phone calls returned.	1	2	3	4	5
I dictate my outgoing letters.	1	2	3	4	5

	YES	USUALLY	SOME	RARELY	NEVER
I look for ways to standardize forms for frequent functions.	1	2	3	4	5
I cluster my return phone calls for one time of day.	1	2	3	4	5
I return phone calls in order of priority.	1	2	3	4	5
I never "dodge" difficult callers.	1	2	3	4	5
I seek out causes of interruptions and try to control them.	1	2	3	4	5
I use non-offensive tactics with long-winded callers.	1	2	3	4	5
I adapt my diary review interval to the severity of the case.	1	2	3	4	5
I phone instead of writing as much as possible.	1	2	3	4	5
I never open my own mail.	1	2	3	4	5
I avoid memos and prefer face-to-face exchanges.	1	2	3	4	5
I plan every out-of-office trip.	1	2	3	4	5
I put my commuting time to good use.	1	2	3	4	5
I have eliminated one time-waster within the past month.	1	2	3	4	5
I feel in control of my time and on top of my job.	1	2	3	4	5
My desk and office are organized and free of clutter.	1	2	3	4	5

	YES	USUALLY	SOME	RARELY	NEVER
I look forward to going to work each morning.	1	2	3	4	5
Each day I tackle the hardest jobs first.	1	2	3	4	5
I defer reviewing my mail if I'm in the middle of something else.	1	2	3	4	5
I contribute questions and ideas to staff meetings.	1	2	3	4	5
I seek from my Supervisor only that information I can't obtain on my own.	1	2	3	4	5
I schedule time with my Supervisor to discuss questions and problems that arise.	1	2	3	4	5
I meet deadlines consistently.	1	2	3	4	5
I am able to control paperwork.	1	2	3	4	5
I think of ways to handle claims more efficiently.	1	2	3	4	5
I make time to regularly read trade journals germane to my job.	1	2	3	4	5
I rarely take work home.	1	2	3	4	5
I make time to be involved in claim associations.	1	2	3	4	5
I am continuing my claims education by taking classes.	1	2	3	4	5
I rarely work on weekends.	1	2	3	4	5

	YES	USUALLY	SOME	RARELY	NEVER
I accept some interruptions as inevitable and try to work around them.	1	2	3	4	5
I rarely receive complaints about late reports or investigations.	1	2	3	4	5

TOTAL SCORE _____

SUPERVISORY/MANAGEMENT APPRAISAL

	YES	USUALLY	SOME	RARELY	NEVER
I keep specific career goals related to advancement.	1	2	3	4	5
I have recorded my time use within the past year.	1	2	3	4	5
I have written objectives and priorities each day.	1	2	3	4	5
I prioritize my "to do" list, starting with the most important.	1	2	3	4	5
I schedule a block of uninterrupted time each day.	1	2	3	4	5
I have eliminated recurring crises.	1	2	3	4	5
I plan my time on a weekly and monthly basis.	1	2	3	4	5

	YES	USUALLY	SOME	RARELY	NEVER
I put travel and waiting time to good use.	1	2	3	4	5
I do not let my staff delegate jobs and problems up to me.	1	2	3	4	5
I do not assign "choice" cases to myself.	1	2	3	4	5
I complete performance appraisals on time.	1	2	3	4	5
I freely delegate to my staff.	1	2	3	4	5
I do not answer questions from my staff that they can answer on their own.	1	2	3	4	5
I work with the receptionist/secretary to help me manage incoming phone calls.	1	2	3	4	5
My "open door" policy does not mean that anyone can interrupt me any time.	1	2	3	4	5
I put telephone time "on hold" to good use.	1	2	3	4	5
I take time each day to do nothing.	1	2	3	4	5
I have little trouble getting my phone calls returned.	1	2	3	4	5
I dictate all outgoing letters.	1	2	3	4	5
I seek ways to standardize forms for frequent use.	1	2	3	4	5

	YES	USUALLY	SOME	RARELY	NEVER
I cluster return phone calls for one time of day.	1	2	3	4	5
I return phone calls in order of priority.	1	2	3	4	5
I never "dodge" difficult callers.	1	2	3	4	5
I think of ways to make staff training more efficient.	1	2	3	4	5
I diagnose causes of interruptions and try to prevent them.	1	2	3	4	5
My meetings have written agendas.	1	2	3	4	5
My meetings begin and end on time.	1	2	3	4	5
I meet with the receptionist periodically to review time-saving ideas.	1	2	3	4	5
I phone instead of write as much as possible.	1	2	3	4	5
I let someone else open my mail.	1	2	3	4	5
I avoid memos, preferring face-to-face exchanges.	1	2	3	4	5
I plan every out-of-office trip.	1	2	3	4	5
I put my commuting time to good use.	1	2	3	4	5
I have specific goals related to management advancement.	1	2	3	4	5

	YES	USUALLY	SOME	RARELY	NEVER
I have eliminated one time-waster within the past month.	1	2	3	4	5
I require my staff to keep written career goals.	1	2	3	4	5
I leave a written agenda before making out-of-town trips.	1	2	3	4	5
I make time for regular marketing and solicitation efforts.	1	2	3	4	5
I feel in control of my time and on top of my job.	1	2	3	4	5
My desk and office are organized and free of clutter.	1	2	3	4	5
I look forward to going to work each morning.	1	2	3	4	5
Each day I tackle the hardest jobs first.	1	2	3	4	5
I defer reviewing my mail if I'm in the middle of something else.	1	2	3	4	5
I have discussed time management problems with my staff in the past month.	1	2	3	4	5
I avoid getting directly involved in an adjuster's cases unless there is a major problem.	1	2	3	4	5
I do not interrupt my staff unless the matter is urgent and can't wait.	1	2	3	4	5

	YES	USUALLY	SOME	RARELY	NEVER
I make time to regularly read trade journals germane to my job.	1	2	3	4	5
I rarely take work home.	1	2	3	4	5
I rarely work weekends.	1	2	3	4	5
I accept some interruptions as inevitable and try to work around them.	1	2	3	4	5

TOTAL SCORE

SCORING EVALUATION

50-99 points. You are already very efficient at managing your time. This book will offer good reinforcement for the sound habits you already possess.

100-149 points. You are selectively efficient, but have some areas of improvement to be a top-flight manager of your claim time.

150-199 points. Don't fret, because this is where most claims professionals find themselves. You may not have given it a lot of thought, but you can be in control of your time by developing new habits.

200-250 points. Good thing you've got this book! You have the largest challenge but also the biggest area for seeing real gains.

Return to this quiz periodically, say every 90 days, to gauge your progress in time-management skills. Invite your claim staff to take it, too.

Chapter Three

Fighting — And Winning — The Paper War

While outsiders often view paperwork as the lifeblood of the insurance industry, paperwork can also foil adjusters' time management attempts. The sheer volume of paperwork which claim professionals are expected to process numbs the mind. Incoming mail is the biggest culprit. Atop this is a seemingly endless stream of office memos, directives from the corporate ivory tower, instructions on new accounts, revised instructions, revisions of the revised instructions, *ad infinitum* if not *ad nauseam.*

Much literature on paperwork control has only limited use for claims professionals. File documentation is crucial and lack thereof may invite E & O situations. Some paperwork must be accepted as inevitable. Still, claim professionals should guard against becoming mere "file documenters" as opposed to loss adjusters.

Despite predictions of paperless offices and file systems, the fact remains that — like it or not — adjusters continue to be inundated by a sizeable volume of paperwork. For instance, Aetna Life & Casualty estimates that it generates a billion documents a year. An Equitable spokesman admits that his company annually churns out a stack of 8 1/2 by 11-inch sheets *six miles high!*[1] As they sang in "The Sound of Music," "...Climb every mountain ..."

Granted, not all of this is claims-related. Much pertains to underwriting, rating, accounting and the like. Nevertheless, one could safely bet that of all sectors of the insurance industry, the Claims Department generates the largest tidal wave of paperwork.

Adjuster boot-camps and training classes fail to prepare the new claims person for this aspect of the job. How could anyone prepare for it? For a trainee in the field just a few months or for a seasoned pro, the paperwork experience can be maddening. We have all felt the same sinking feeling in the pit of our stomachs when a pound of mail is dumped on our desks. Somehow, claim professionals must manage it: read some, act upon some others, file some away, route some to the trash bin. New adjusters often find this disillusioning, since certain personal organizational skills are either taken for granted or are given a low priority in training programs.

These same adjusters, fresh from the adjusting training school, often complain, "Paper-shuffle, paper-shuffle."

Even from the ranks of mid-level management one picks up sarcastic references to the "Memo re Memo re Memo ..." as they read and initial till kingdom come. Whomever portrayed the study of *law* as a "paper chase" could have selected the claims industry as a more appropriate setting. Yet, it always feels like the *paper* is chasing *us!*

A TV commercial for a large office supply corporation portrays an executive completing dictation by remarking, "... and a copy to every sales manager, Ms. Jones." Like so many snowflakes from the sky, the papers begin falling, descending on the alarmed executive. By the commercial's end, the desk-bound executive is literally up to his neck in paper as he desperately screams, "Ms. Jones!!!" Claim professionals could have produced this commercial.

Unless they become overwhelmed by a tsunami of paper, claim professionals must have an overall strategy and specific tactics for "winning the paper war." Let's face it, adjusters are paid to handle and close claims. To an extent, some modicum of paperwork is needed to meet this goal. Past a point, though, excess paperwork gets out of control and can keep claim professionals from accomplishing much. Paperwork can bleed precious time that could otherwise be spent investigating, evaluating and negotiating claims. Some guiding principles in keeping paperwork under control:

Tip #1 Face the Music

Essentially there are two ways to defeat the paperwork monster: control the source or control the effects. Sources are things over which claims professionals may have very little control. Some paper is vital to your job. The claims business is a people- and paper-intensive field. You *need* those voluminous in-patient hospital records, even if they are 200 pages thick. There's no way to keep people from writing to you. You cannot tell your boss or your home office to please stop sending you memos. As the saying goes, "you can run but you can't hide." There is little one can do to dam up the font from which the paper river flows.

One can, however, use systematic techniques to handle the paper we process every day. All it takes is an awareness of certain strategies and tactics and, most importantly, a willingness to change ingrained habits. A small investment of time on paperwork management techniques will repay itself many times over in one's career — regardless of employer or field.

Let's begin with the biggest foe, the daily mail barrage.

Tip #2: Sort Mail Promptly

Federal Express is not alone in its dislike of the U.S. Postal Service. In many insurance offices, arrival of the mail is met with a dread usually reserved for a trip to the dentist.

Don't kill the messenger. Instead, discipline yourself to sort mail promptly. After the mail is opened and distributed, sort each day's mail as it arrives and match it to the appropriate file. If you have some clerical or "claim tech" help for this, then all the better! If you do not have the file, find it or ask someone to track it down for you. Avoid letting a backup of loose mail to accumulate on your desk, in the drawer, or on the floor. Otherwise, soon there will be so much clutter that there will be no place to work. This creates a vicious cycle: as the clutter pile grows, so does the temptation to put off organizing it. Failure to promptly match mail with its respective file can have disastrous claims-handling consequences as well.

Tip #3: Handle Each Piece Just Once

Try to handle each piece of mail just once. For example, with your pen, make a small dot in the lower right corner of the letter so you can monitor the number of times you handle each piece of paper. If the paper develops a case of the measles, that's a sign that maybe you're not handling the paper-flow as efficiently as you could. If you receive a request for some item in your file, reply to it then. If a client wants a status report, get it behind you while it is fresh on your mind. Handle correspondence as it arrives. Do not wait to reply just because it hasn't yet "come up on diary." Avoid the temptation to cram a letter in your file just because it's in your way and you feel that you'll deal with it when the file comes up on diary. This, however, should be tempered with the following practice ...

Tip #4: "Prioritize" Your Mail

What is this? Most people are conditioned to dealing with mail sequentially, that is in the same order it arrived. This is a poor approach to handling mail, though. Distinguish the relative importance of the paper you receive each day. Management consultant Jane Brody explains her technique:

> "Sort your mail each morning into three piles— that which must be done immediately, that which can wait awhile, and that which can be filed or discarded. Take care of the "immediate" pile and clear the rest from your desk, so you're not constantly reminded of how behind you are."[2]

Scan the mail and focus on those items warranting immediate attention. The rest may be diaried or placed in the file. Examples of priority correspondence might include:

> "Attached please find suit papers..."
> "If I do not hear from you within ten days, I will file suit..."
> "Trial is scheduled two weeks from today. Please follow up to..."
> "Reserves now exceed Home Office reporting threshold. Report immediately to..."
> "Please provide a status report on..."

Good claim supervisors will try to highlight priority correspondence, but this is a trait which each adjuster can and should develop. Certain words are tip-offs as to the urgency of the correspondence:

- "overdue"
- "file suit"
- "impending trial"
- "immediate attention"
- "bad faith"

Isolate the day's most important correspondence; organize the remainder. Get the non-urgent items in their respective files and attack the rest.

Mail with moderate urgency might include:

- *reserve change suggestions*
- *letters from lawyers transmitting medical information*
- *medical bills from claimants*

Mail with low to zero priority would include:

- *advertising literature from vendors*
- *promotional material*
- *publications which no longer hold any use for you*

Similarly, flag and prioritize your *own* outgoing letters. Have an office supply store prepare for you some rubber stamps of frequently-used expressions: "Reply Requested," "Suit Papers Attached," "Second Request," "Bull$*%^" (just kidding, there), etc. Use them on appropriate correspondence. This will flag the attention of the recipient and save you time that would otherwise be spent following up. This will save recipients time too, since they don't have to slog through six pages of report to determine if an immediate response is needed.

Tip #5: Use the "Boomerang" Technique

You don't have to live down under, mate, to use an old aborigine tactic. This is useful for letters which include space for a reply. Minimize paperwork and reduce turnaround time on these items warranting a prompt response. Hand-write your answer at the bottom, make a photocopy for your file and then send it on its way. Indicate on your reply note that you've kept a copy, or have a rubber stamp prepared with this notation, so the other person won't think you're dismissing the sender's idea.

Redundant requests for status reports which crossed in the mail, form requests from Compensation Commissions, some correspondence from other insurance carriers — these are examples of letters which can be bounced back to the sender. Hence the term, "boomerang" effect. Before you can say, "G'day mate," the paper will be moving away from you. For letters not needing a formal or dictated reply and for which a very brief comment will suffice, this technique may save you much time.

Follow the "Three D's"

Employ the "three D's" tactic best described by Robert Weingarten, publisher of *Financial World*. His motto: "Do it, delegate it or ditch it."[3] Yes, the lowly wastebasket can be a super paper management tool. Some time management consultants recommend that a trash can be nearby whenever going through your daily mail. Regardless of whether you are the first in the office to review or open the mail, a trash can is one of the best tools you can have. Envelopes, duplicative correspondence, junk mail — discard these items at once, saving time, not to mention saving clutter from overtaking your files. Not all time-saving devices have to be high-tech! Let's recap these three D's:

Tip #6: Do!

"*Do it!*" For priority mail, examples of which have been noted, these should be your guiding words.

Tip #7: Delegate!

"*Delegate it!*" Adjusters may feel that there is very little they can actually delegate. Most likely, they are delegated to rather than the ones doing the delegating. Still, much mail can be relegated to the file immediately or deferred to the future by placing them on diary. Claim supervisors and managers can delegate to assistants, a clerical person or a secretary.

Tip #8: Ditch!

"*Ditch it!*" This can include more items of redundant correspondence (e.g., medical reports, bills, etc.) than you think. In auditing claim files, it is amazing to see the amount of duplicative material: two or more copies of the same medical report, bill, legal report, etc. Why file this excess baggage? Put your claim files on Slim-Fast!

Get your name removed from mailing lists of little-read periodicals or publications. Be ruthless in throwing away duplicative correspondence or paper you don't need.

Tip #9: Establish a Quiet Hour

Say that again? Some adjusters may wonder, "*What* quiet hour?" Nevertheless, every office has certain slower times of day, just as some days or times of year are busier or slower. Increasingly, companies institute a "quiet hour" for all employees at one point during the work day. I have been in a claim department at the Hanover Insurance Company where adjuster calls were not put through until 10:00 a.m. During this time, no outgoing calls are made and all incoming calls are "held." The purpose was to afford some uncluttered time for planning, organizing and generally "sharpening the saw."

Adjusters can devote this hour to "thought work" rendered impossible by the telephone's incessant ring. Unfortunately, this is a luxury few offices are willing to taste. As a service business, claims departments must be accessible. If they aren't, business will suffer. Improved time management is pointless if it alienates callers or clients.

If office or company policy prohibits a quiet hour, then adjusters must simply work around the problem by observing those hours which are quietest and most conducive to handling paperwork without interruption. Generally, there are three such times: before the office officially opens in the morning; during lunch hour; after the office officially closes for the day. Assuming you do not wish to go in earlier or work later, you may consider taking a "working lunch."

Tip #10: Schedule "Afternoon Delight"

No, this is not what you might think. Consider taking your lunch to work, or buying it and bringing it back to your office. During a working lunch, you may wish to have in-coming calls held. (Adjusters may need to stagger their lunch hours so there is always someone available to accept new assignments, handle problems, etc.) Mid-day is often an excellent time to handle incoming mail, quickly answer correspondence, return routine phone calls, get organized and to clear the desk of any rubble inevitably accumulated during the average morning. (Another plus: you'll save *money* by "brown-bagging" too!)

Lunch at 1 p.m. instead of noon. This is often a quieter time of day. You also avoid the noon-time lunch rush and save yourself some time.

Do not skip lunch, though! You must keep your energy level high to handle claims. You need a change of scene once and a while to refresh yourself and clear your head. Get up and stretch, walk around or get outside for a few minutes. A break may be just what you need to relieve some tension and return you to the office a more efficient person. Thus, a good time management technique for adjusters is to consciously schedule some time each day to "take a breather."

> *Betty handled 250 serious workers' compensation claims and felt tremendous stress, a feeling shared by many other adjusters in her same office. Each day at lunch she walked one mile around the nicely landscaped office park surrounding her company's office. Soon other adjusters joined her for the mid-day walk and they returned to the office mentally and physically refreshed.*

This is not meant to be a stress management manual for claims people, although they could certainly use such guidance! Time- and stress-management overlap, however, in that managing stress makes one more efficient in the use of time.

Do not confuse a working lunch with a business lunch. Business lunches are often time-wasters, consuming two or more hours, three or more martinis. Usually you end up feeling sluggish because you've eaten more than normal. By all means, entertain clients or take them to lunch. This is a useful part of doing business. Just don't allow the practice to get out of hand. Be wary of "freebies" from vendors who would take you to lunch to have you buy their services: law firms, rehab agencies, detective outfits, etc. They may have wonderful products or services, but indulging in the lunch circuit on their tab wastes a lot of time. It also risks potential conflict of interest problems in terms of feeling beholden to particular vendors since they did take you to an expensive French restaurant...

Tip #11: Don't Take it Home

Workaholism is not a sign of time management, but rather a frequent sign of time *mis*management. A bulging briefcase is a sign of poor paper flow management. Avoid constantly taking paperwork home. Some people have a martyr complex and love to moan to others about the work they took home. Some companies have a "corporate culture" which seems to make a contest of who arrives earliest and works latest. If you find yourself constantly taking work home with you, consider delegating more and/or retooling your approach to paperwork management. You need some time away from work and with your family to clear your head and make you more efficient during work hours.

> *Supervisor Del Shaeffer felt a twinge of pride when confessing to people that he was a "workaholic." Del lived, breathed and ate his work. He personally opened and read each piece of incoming mail. He encouraged an "open door" policy where adjusters could walk right into his office to discuss claims. These often became long-winded sessions wherein Del reminisced about "the way things were," last weekend's football game or the weather. Del prided himself on being a "people person" and "having his fingers in many pies." He worked late and office morale began to wane. A promising young adjuster had recently resigned, citing his inability to get questions answered.*

Taking work home undermines your effectiveness while at work in another way. Psychologically, it may cause you to feel "there's no reason for me to get it done today, because I can take it home." Adjusters sometimes cannot avoid taking work home or working during times that most people would call "after hours." When this becomes routine, however, it's time to step back and reassess your approach to paperwork management.

Tip #12: Use a Diary System

There is a fourth "D" regarding paperwork management: the *di*ary. Get some type of desk diary or calendar. Nowadays there are dozens of choices. The local office supply store should have a wide variety. DayRunner is very popular. Filofax and Letts of London make deluxe versions, if you prefer hand-stitched cowhide and inlaid gold embossing. Day Timers is my personal favorite. Make sure it has time slots for each day as well as plenty of room for listing specific targets for the day. You not only want to include your appointments but also the files or tasks you want to work on that day.

When you're finished with a file, page ahead on your calendar and make a note for that date on which you want to follow up. Then send the file on for filing. The claim file is now "on diary." Within a few weeks you should be able to tell which files are coming up for review or action in the future. Lawyers call this a "tickler system" and use it to avoid letting statutes of limitation pass, filing deadlines slip by, etc. Whatever you call it, using a diary system will help you manage paper flow.

Tip #13: Prepare Tomorrow's Schedule Today

Prepare tomorrow's schedule *before* you get to the office. This way, it is less likely that the pseudo-urgent will intrude and grab your attention from needed tasks. Start each day with a list of things to do. For example, when you get to your desk tomorrow morning on the calendar page for that day may be:

✓ report on files 43998, 47002, 39786, 50079, & 44760
✓ f/u w/attny Nields on Sherman case
✓ S/S Buck on Fields loss
✓ damage inspections on Cheyenne Ct.
✓ activity check on Cherokee

Before the end of each work day, page ahead and make sure the following day is mapped out, leaving enough breathing room for inevitable "unforeseeables." This brings us to our next tip...

Tip #14: Do Not "Over-Diary"

Adapt the interval between diary reviews to the needs of the case. A workers' comp file involving nothing but paying out a permanent partial disability award may be able to go 120 days between reviews. A large fire loss at a manufacturing site needs to be reviewed once a week or even daily. Think about the diary interval needed so you won't be awash in files.

> *"An examiner must be careful to make the diary reflect the needs of the individual case... A case which need not be seen more than once a month should not be put on a diary for semi-monthly review. Certainly, a case which needs review every two weeks should not be on a monthly diary basis."*[4]

Adjusters more often err on the side of under-diarying or not using a diary system at all. It is possible to go too far in the opposite extreme, however. Avoid painting yourself into a corner and wasting a lot of time with needless file-handling by over-diarying.

Tip #15: Use the Mail as an Ally

If you are swamped with work, use the mail as an alternative to spinning wheels. If urgency is not a top priority, and if five to six days will not compromise the quality of the investigation, then use the mail instead. Examples: Write for an accident report instead of driving downtown and waiting in line at the Police Station. Send a written request for a medical report you need. A quick hand-written letter consumes a fraction of the time it takes to drive somewhere. Don't get mad at the mail, get even! Use the mail to your own advantage as a timesaving device.

Field adjusters take lots of photographs: accident scenes, damaged cars, burnt property, injuries, etc. Rather than driving to and from the Fotomat or drug store for developing, use one of the many photo processing by mail services. Many of these outfits will give you service as fast as any of the "drive-to" places. Another bonus: they are often less expensive than the "drive-to" stores.

Tip #16: Let Someone Else Open The Mail

Don't be the one who opens your office's mail. Resist this temptation. In most claim offices, opening and sorting mail is a clerical task, which it is and should be. Minutes can be added to your day by refusing to succumb to the desire to see your mail first. I have worked in some claim offices where the Claims Manager opened all the mail. Perhaps this was just a compulsive habit. Captain Queeg constantly fiddled with steel balls too. Both habits waste time.

Tip #17: Trash It

Master the art of "wastebasketry" and use the trash can as a management tool. It may not be as high-tech as a Hayes Modem, but it can be effective. If you must be the first to review and open the office mail, keep a trash can nearby. Envelopes, duplicative correspondence, junk mail — these items can be discarded at once, saving time as well as space in the file jackets.

Tip #18: Be a "Fingertip" Manager

Keep needed forms well within reach and let your fingers do the walking. If you frequently use particular forms, keep an ample supply on hand in a desk drawer or otherwise within reach. Preferably, this should *not* be atop of your desk. Storing frequently-used forms saves time from needless trips to the supply area looking for a form. It saves you from distractions you might encounter while walking to the supply area like, "Hey Judy, did you see this new case I just got?" Keeping all your needed materials close by is "fingertip management." If you do this, you may feel less inclined to give the postal carrier the finger.

- Damage appraisers need to keep close at hand crash books, NADA valuation guides, calculators and estimation forms.
- Property loss adjusters may keep at their desks a calculator, phone numbers of salvage dealers, contractors and wholesalers.
- Adjusters handling auto claims will need templates and rulers for drawing diagrams of accident scenes.

Keep a small desk clock nearby as well. This will make you more time-conscious and will help keep you from losing track of time.

One management study found that the average executive wastes nearly four work-weeks a year because things are misplaced, misfiled, mislabeled—or just missing![5] Don't become one of them!

Tip #19: Organize Your Work Area

Do you still really believe that a clean desk is a sign of a sick mind? Are you the type who says, "I know what it looks like but I know where everything is."? (Why don't neatniks sport signs saying, "A sloppy desk is a sign of a sloppy person"?) Once again, organization gets a bad rap. Get your desk organized! That does not necessarily mean squeaky-clean. Clear away obstructions that keep you from working efficiently. Establish "desk files" for items you frequently need and use for reference. At least every six months, review your desk files and purge them of unwanted, unused or out-dated material. This helps keep you from drowning in paper. Keep an ample stock of office supplies you need. Try to keep but one file on your desk at a time.

Before leaving your desk at the end of the work day, make sure your In-basket is empty and that your desk is cleared and ready for the next work day. Nothing is as demoralizing as coming into the office in the morning and seeing your desk covered with yesterday's clutter. Start the day on a strong, positive note. Before you leave, clear your desk of files, notes and messages, and organize them. Clear your In-basket so you can "hit the ground running" the next day.

Keep only one In-basket on your desk. A variation of Parkinson's Law applies here: paper will expand to fill the time and space available for it. Multiple In-baskets somehow become paper magnets. Pare it down to one and perhaps people will not be as tempted to dump things in it!

Organizing the work space for optimum efficiency has become a legitimate management topic in its own right. (For further reading, try *The Successful Office: How to Create a Workspace,* by Franklin Becker.) You don't have to be ready for a white-glove inspection. Your office surrounding need not be antiseptic. Be comfortable in your work environment but be organized. Don't get too wrapped up in office furnishings, though. Over-concern with office trappings is a sign of misplaced priorities and can quickly get out of hand.

Tip #20: Keep Reference Material Close By

Keep reference materials at your desk or at a nearby bookcase and start building your own time-saving reference library: dictionary, medical dictionary, law dictionary, **Physicians Desk Reference**, phone directories, (a copy of **Time Management for Claims Professionals**), local physicians directory, local claims association directory, reference texts on your line of adjusting, etc. Develop your own reference files for information you frequently need: lists of local contractors, salvage dealers, rental car companies, structures settlement firms, engineer-consultants, etc. This will save you many scavenger hunts.

Tip #21: Standardize Forms

Certain items of correspondence that you send over and over should be standardized so that all you have to do is to fill in the blanks and save yourself time. A word processor helps greatly in this regard, but even if your office doesn't have one you can save a lot of time that would otherwise be spent writing, drafting or dictating. Examples of letters and forms which can be routinized to a great degree:

- Acknowledgement letters to claimant lawyers;
- Letters to medical providers requesting medical records and bills;
- Letter to doctors for independent medical exams;
- "Please call me" letters to claimants and witnesses; and
- Correspondence to compensation commissions regarding filings.

Develop your own "homemade" forms if you see a need that your company's stock forms do not meet. Check-off type forms are great for this purpose. Work with a secretary to develop a sample check-off form then run off some copies and *voila*, you're in business. At my company, we specialize in product liability claims for medical device manufacturers. We have developed an inventory of over sixty different types of correspondence that we use for every conceivable situation pertaining to product liability defense. Consider what you can do on other types of claims to avoid recomposing letters and reinventing the wheel repeatedly.

Another tactic is to develop your own notebook of "stock" paragraphs. Use a three-ring binder for this purpose. Chances are you have seen letters you have admired from other people. These "zingers" may be from attorneys, other insurance companies or adjusters whose writing you emulate. Some of your best correspondence may be good examples and form part of this "Greatest Hits" collection. If there are certain recurring types of paragraphs which crop up, keep a notebook of the best examples and use them as guidelines when dictating.

Tip #22: Avoid "Memo Mania"

The death knell of much productive time has been the phrase, "Read and initial." Some people (and you probably know who they are) seem to generate a stream of memos that not even an Evelyn Wood valedictorian could scan in a single day. Some adjusters say that there are two classes of people in this regard: those who have too little time to read them and those who seem to write too many of them. Memos are written communication meant for someone within your organization. Anything written for someone outside your organization is a letter.

A few years ago the following memo was spotted in the U.S. Department of Energy office of Washington D.C.:

NOTICE

To make things easier for all of us, please notice this important notice about notices. You may have noticed the increased amount of notices for you to notice. We notice that some of our notices have not been noticed. This is very noticeable! It is noticed that the responses to the notices have been noticeably unnoticeable. This notice is to remind you to notice the notices because we do not want the notices to go unnoticed.

(Signed)
Notice Committee for Noticing Notices

Leave it to the federal bureaucrats!

Client instructions, benefit policies, unmatched mail addressed to you for unknown reasons — these are telltale signs of memo-mania. Little can be done to stem the tide of memos. Many memos do not require careful reading. On the other hand, if everyone genuinely took the time to read each and every memo, very little work would get done.

Start by setting an example. Avoid generating memos. If you've got something to say to another person, say it, don't write it. Lots of folks within the same organization sitting around writing memos to each other is a sign that people aren't really communicating. Don't be an offender. Be judicious in your use of memos.

Tip #23: Exploit the Power of E-Mail

More and more offices have electronic mail (e-mail). This has a number of good qualities. It can facilitate communication among staffs. It can also provide a forum for frank discussion. It can minimize the amount of hard-copy paper floating around.

Like any form of communication, though, e-mail can be abused as well as used. Unfortunately, there are folks who are so taken with the novelty of e-mail that they over-use it. For example, some people always "cc" the boss or supervisor on any memo as a CYA strategy. E-mail may spur the proliferation of superfluous information, adding to the already burgeoning state of information overload.

Some beleaguered bosses — such as Microsoft's Bill Gates — have installed a so-called Bozo-filter, in order to screen e-mail from all but their closest friends and business associates. This may be extreme, but it shows how new technologies can be a double-edged sword in terms of time management ... or mismanagement.

Tip #24: Get the Fax

Get a facsimile ("fax") or telecopier machine if your clients have them and you're sending out a lot of claim reports and correspondence. Fax machines let you transmit and receive reports almost instantaneously using the phone lines. This saves you much money that would otherwise be spent using overnight express delivery services. A fax will not necessarily reduce your paperwork, but it may give you some extra time within which to prepare reports, etc. since you no longer have to build three days of mail time into your calculations. Virtually all businesses now have fax machines, however, so they give your claim office an extra dimension of service.

Remember the vision of paper-less claims offices?

Not so fast! For one thing, the vision has sputtered due in part to the ubiquitous fax machine. A Gallup poll published in April 1994 revealed the adjuster's worst nightmare — we're ALL faxed to the max!

Evidence:

- the average Fortune 500 location has 19 fax machines, up from 16 in 1993;
- fax transmissions account for 36% of a Fortune 500 firm's yearly phone bill — $3.75 million to $5 million;
- typical users fax 207 pages daily — 41 documents of about five pages apiece.

Though more business people are using e-mail, faxing is often easier and cost-effective. Is our productivity enhanced by all this high-tech communications? Probably not. Priority Management, a consulting firm, estimates that an average worker has 36 hours of work stacked on the desk, but only 90 minutes to spend on it. (USA Today, April 20, 1994, p. A1, "Faxes Taxing Office Life"). Yikes! Here are some tips on maximizing the time-saving use of fax:

Tip #25: Hand-Write Your Replies

If you receive a fax which seeks a reply, hand-write your reply on the bottom and fax it back to the sender. There is no requirement that replies be typed or dictated.

Tip #26: Fax = Urgent ... *Incorrect!!!*

Don't assume that it's urgent or important just because it came by fax. Some lawyers and others may think they are impressing you by faxing correspondence which could just have easily arrived by regular mail. Resist the temptation to drop everything and read a fax, just because it's a fax. Ask yourself, "Is this genuinely urgent or important?"

> *QUINLEY'S TIME MANAGEMENT AXIOM #64:*
> The urgent is not necessarily important;
> the important is often not urgent.

Tip #27: Train the Fax Fetishist

If you're getting a lot of non-urgent faxes, educate the senders. For example, if attorneys you are working with think they're impressing you, let them know that they ARE ... in a *negative* way. (Decline to pay for any fax or line charges for non-urgent transmissions.) Nor are defense lawyers the only abusers. At times, I've had to tell a claimant attorney, "Let's give the fax machines a rest." Discourage those who seem to have a fax fetish. Also, let them know that just because it came by fax does not necessarily mean that you will answer by fax or treat the communication as urgent. One bad aspect to fax is that it often creates an expectation of split-second reply on the part of the sender. Set the sender straight.

Tip #28: Screen Incoming Faxes

Have someone else screen incoming faxes to assess whether they are truly urgent. Faxes of a "for reporting purposes" nature can be filed in the claim jacket. Others requesting authority, decisions, containing threats and deadlines do warrant prompt attention and should not be deferred until the next diary.

Tip #29: Join "Over-Faxers Anonymous"

Make sure that you're not an offender here. Take care that the faxes you send are genuinely urgent and important. Just because the letter came to you by fax, it doesn't necessarily follow that your reply must be by fax.

Tip #30: Delegate the "Send Fax" Function

Avoid sending the fax yourself. If possible, delegate this to a support person. Is it the best use of your time standing next to the fax machine, waiting for it to "send"? On the other hand, if it's 5:45 p.m., your secretary has left and you need something to go out, go ahead and take matters into your own hands. Don't be too proud (or ignorant) to operate the fax machine if you need something sent and there's no support staff in sight.

Tip #31: Package Your Message to Grab Attention

If your office has a personal computer and your clients do too, consider sending reports, messages and correspondence by mailgrams or telegrams. Western Union has an Easy-Link service that specializes in this. If you have a PC, you will need a modem to send messages over the telephone line. This will reduce paper, be quicker than relying on the mails and may impress you client with your split-second efficiency.

Tip #32: Become a Speed-Skimmer

Claims professionals must constantly read. Medical reports, insurance policies and legal analyses all demand close attention. Not all correspondence requires total and immediate concentration, but it takes time to develop a "sixth sense" about this. One technique: glance briefly over a memo to see if it involves anything of immediate concern to you or your work. If so, read it carefully and pass it on. If not, skim over it and make a mental note to consult the memo, company instructional folder, etc., should you ever need to pursue the topic further. You can always call Evelyn Wood and become a speed-reader too.

Tip #33: Call — Don't Write

The average business letter costs over $25 to send. Before dictating or sending out any letter, ask yourself, "Could this be handled by phone?" If so, call, don't write. Chances are it takes less time, especially if all you're looking for is a "yes or no" response. Don't hide behind correspondence. Discussions about proposals or disagreements over claim evaluations are often better handled orally than on paper. Call — don't write, and encourage others you deal with to do the same. (*Do* document you phone discussions in your claim progress sheets, but look for ways to use the phone to reduce paper.)

Tip #34: Keep it Moving

Do you ever feel like you're playing tennis against six opponents on the opposite side of the net, each one hitting a ball toward you and demanding that you play only with him? With the daily barrage of in-coming paper, the claims professional quickly feels this way. Get the memo clutter off your desk.

Do what you can to re-route the paper flood. Read that memo, initial it and pass it on. Hand that file to the clerk with instructions to draw the indemnity draft. Read those new client instructions and place them in the instruction book. In short, get the mound *off* your desk. Knock the ball into the other guy's court. Or, get some more players on *your* side of the court!

Tip #35: Don't Be a Collector

Are you a closet pack-rat? Or, have you come out of the closet? Whenever reviewing a memo, ask yourself, "If I really needed this information some day, could I retrieve it?" If the answer is "yes," then maybe a quick glance-over of the memo would be in order. Avoid the temptation to let this material pile up. As with anything else, the higher the paperwork pile, the greater the temptation to avoid tackling the problem at all. Memos can quickly cause this snowball effect if left uncontrolled from the outset.

Tip #36: ... or a Piler

The piler gets to the paperwork when, uh, well, when he gets to it. Monday's mail may be lucky to get sorted by Thursday. One sure-fire way exists to spot the piler: the Leaning Tower of Pisa In-Basket. The piler's desk appears to be (and is) a hopeless morass of paper, in which the piler is mired. Usually, the piler has other things to do, which means that the job of organizing is deferred to the never-never land of the future. Naturally, the higher the pile grows, the greater the temptation to procrastinate on further attempts to organize the mound of mail, memos and the like.

Pilers are endangered species due to their high visibility. Their disorganization attracts the attention of supervisors or managers who (for good reason) do not tolerate the practice. Pilers have various ways of confronting this challenge. Sometimes they insist that despite their apparent disorganization, they know just where everything is. More often than not, this is simply rationalization. Like Lon Chaney who became a Werewolf under the full moon, pilers will occasionally transform themselves into squirrels, about which we will discuss more later. This metamorphosis does not solve the problem but is an attempt to camouflage it.

After considerable pressure, pilers will sometimes change. Pilers often like to complain about the volume of paperwork when they should be spending more time organizing it, working it down.

Woe be unto the time management effort of any claims professional afflicted with this kind of case of "the piles." See your claims doctor for an organizational remedy!

Tip #37: ... or a Squirrel

Into this taxonomy falls many reformed pilers who have learned the hard way that those piles incur supervisory wrath. The squirrel does get the clutter off the desk. That is good! The squirrel does *not* take time to organize the clutter. The squirrel deposits it in some out of the way cubbyhole in the desk, always presumably meaning to get to it "eventually." This is bad!

Squirrels are usually caught by the apoplectic supervisor who has happened upon the desk drawer of one of his or her adjusters, only to find a three-inch stack of unmatched mail dating back over two months. "Out of sight — out of mind." The squirrel never does get around to organizing the paper. The disorganization remains, but is made less visible by transferring the problem from the desk top to some nook or cranny. This problem may go undetected until the discerning supervisor comes across the cache of unmatched correspondence, mail or memos.

Prior to diagnosis and apprehension, squirrels themselves often forget about their hidden treasure. Again, out of sight — out of mind. Through such forgetfulness they often labor under no guilt about what they *should* have done. Unlike pilers, squirrels are not as consistently or as vividly reminded of the need to get organized. Due to the greater resourcefulness of hiding techniques, squirrels may survive longer and remain undetected longer than pilers.

Tip #38: ... or a "Deep-Sixer"

At first blush, the deep-sixer appears to have no problem. Deep-sixers are meticulous in ensuring that each piece of mail goes immediately into its respective file each day. Sometimes, but not often, the deep-sixer even reads the mail. In such selectivity lies the deep-sixer's problem. While the deep-sixer is not victimized by clutter, he stands to get burned by not acting promptly on some correspondence he immediately interred in the file jacket. For the deep-sixer, as the name implies, is indiscriminate: everything goes at once into the file: medical reports with return-to-work dates, routine correspondence, suit papers. Presumably these will be attended to on the next diary date.

Risks run by the deep-sixer are those errors-and-omissions nightmares of default judgments, hastily-prepared litigation defenses, overpayment of claims and client complaints. The deep-sixer's problem is one more subtle than that of the piler or the squirrel. While the deep-sixer has avoided the clutter problem, he is too indiscriminate in handling paperwork and mail. He fails to set priorities on each day's mail. Hence he sits astride a ticking time-bomb. Not each piece of mail can be consigned to the file jacket until the diary date arrives, although the deep-sixer acts as though this were the case.

Supervisors will find it more difficult still to spot and reform deep-sixers, since they outwardly seem to be well-organized. Diagnosis of the problem can be made through a close reading of files. Identify those priority items of correspondence, check the date-stamp, and make sure that the file reflects the date of activity pertaining to the correspondence. In some cases, this may require the supervisor to ask the adjuster, "How do you handle the mail each day?" Whenever the adjuster places the sanctity of the diary date above the exigencies of prompt and appropriate claims-handling, a deep-sixer has emerged.

Tip #39: Explore Scanning to Reduce Paper

Maybe the idea of the paperless office isn't so unattainable after all. Optical scanners — both hand-held and flatbed — are rapidly dropping in price. These allow you to "download" papers to a hard drive or some other form of media storage. While there is some paper which you must retain in its original form, optical scanning holds some promise in helping claim offices minimize hard copy storage and organize retrieval. Within a few years, it may be customary for each adjuster, or at least adjusting office, to have a scanner to minimize space and storage requirements.

Tip #40: Visualize the Benefits

Rewards are many for the claims professionals who change old habits and adopt a no-nonsense, common sense approach to handling the daily influx of mail. As in every aspect of time management, it is one thing to know what needs to be done and quite another to break old habits and do it. Knowing means nothing without *doing*.

Unattended paperwork tends to snowball. Ignored correspondence begets more correspondence, each subsequent item more strident than the last. The more correspondence that one ignores or sloughs off, the more likely that more letters will follow. Bad breeds bad, and good breeds good. The more mail that piles up, the greater is the temptation to procrastinate further. The vicious cycle must be broken at some point. Few shortcuts are available. Time invested in managing paperwork will repay itself many times over, and will avert or break the snowball effect of "the paperwork blizzard."

Much of the claim professional's job involves reporting to clients or to other offices on claim status. To a degree, daily mail is a barometer as to the quality of an adjuster's case-handling. While there is no substitute for an effective diary system, incoming mail can act as a second-line detection method for any work items which have fallen "off diary." However much we try to prevent this, small crises arise. To act as a backup safeguard and to ensure timely reports, there must be some overall strategy as well as specific tactics to hack through the tangle of the paperwork jungle.

Nor can one's mental attitude toward the job remain positive when one feels dread and hopelessness produced by the paperwork morass. Does anyone really enjoy working in the shadow of a rising mound of paper? Is the best part of your day over when the alarm goes off? Does any claims professional actually like feeling guilty about the mail that has been hoarded away somewhere in the desk? Does anyone savor the anxiety that comes with wondering which case is going to "blow up" next because some vital letter was entombed prematurely in the file? Accept the reality that the paper will not go away. Strive to master it, or it will surely master you.

No pat formula exists for determining the urgency or priority of a given letter. Like much of claims handling itself, judgment calls are needed. No substitute exists for experience, but there is no reason why adjusters should be expected to learn how to manage paperwork by the seat of their pants (or skirts). To the extent the claims professional manages the mail and does not let the mail manage him, there will be a more productive individual who feels better about himself and the job. Better to have a system and risk an occasional glitch than to have no system for coping at all.

Armed with an overall view of the paperwork problem and specific principles for handling it, the claims professional need no longer view each day's mail drop with fear and loathing.

NOTES

1. Andrew Tobias, *The Invisible Bankers*. New York: The Linden Press, 1982, p. 23.

2. "Readers Say," *Forbes*. June 9, 1980, p. 20.

3. Neil Carter, *A Guide to Workers' Compensation Claims*. New York: Roberts Publishing Corp., 1978, p. 45.

4. Study of Sanford Teller Communications, New York, June 30, 1986.

Chapter Four

Taming The Telephone

Alright, time to get down to work.

You just sat down to dictate that important report which you have planned for over a week. The investigation is complete, your materials organized on your desk, and the report outline is fixed in your mind. As the third word leaves your mouth and enters the dictaphone, your train of thought and speech is cut short by the receptionist, announcing that you have a call on Line #2.

As you "temporarily" turn from your recorder, you field the phone call, this one from an irate claimant: "Hey #$%@&^ — when in the *&%# are you gonna' see my car!?!?" While engaged with the irate claimant, who forgot to give you his name (he assumes you have but one file—*his*), the receptionist hands you notes stating that you have calls holding for you on three other lines.

Meanwhile, four files requiring your review are tossed atop your in-basket, which starts to resemble the Leaning Tower of Pisa. Also, now waiting at your office door are two adjuster trainees, seeking answers to questions on their claim files. As you return the receiver to its cradle the phone's melodious ring again pierces your eardrum with its urgent message. By the way, can you please review and sign these twenty drafts?

Before you can say "interruption," you have handled six in-coming phone calls, scanned two pounds of incoming mail and have answered five questions. It's 5:00 p.m. already, and you're late for an evening appointment and running further behind. That ambitious "To-Do" list which you prepared last night has very few tasks crossed off. In short, you have accomplished nothing toward what you had planned. How time flies when you're ... chasing files! Are you having fun yet?

Two hours later — stuck in traffic and feeling frustrated — you scratch your head, sift through the rubble, and wonder what it was you were trying to do before the telephone intruded.

The telephone's tyranny transforms this scenario into the claims professional's daily nightmare. Some rare vengeance wreaked by Ma Bell? Hardly. Rather the telephone — while indispensable to the claims-person's job — can also become the adjuster's Number One Headache. In turn, this can produce the adjuster's fantasy: applying a sledgehammer to the telephone receiver!

While telephones improve efficiency, they also spawn new pressures and interruptions. (Some stock brokerage houses now expect employees to handle a call every minute and a half.) Imagine how difficult claims handling would be without the telephone. For instance, cases would simply not turn over as fast, since everything would have to be handled by mail or in person. More personnel would be needed to handle the same amount of claims, producing much inefficiency. Even in the "good old days" relived by many veterans — to whom the recorded statement remains a modern invention — the telephone is an invaluable claims-handling tool.

It is fine and well for the older geezers of the industry to rail about how adjusters should get off the phone and spend their time out of the office investigating claims. Realistically, however, few if any claim professionals have this luxury. One cannot simply unplug the phone any more than we can become Luddites, taking statements with quill pens, inkwells and horse-drawn buggies. (There doesn't seem to be a huge market for Amish-style loss adjusting, anyway.) No one can deny that the adjusting process would be tremendously cumbersome without the telephone.

For good or ill, telephone adjusting is here to stay. With rising cost-consciousness within the insurance industry, telephone adjusting may be the way of the future. As it cuts into your time, however, the telephone is a double-edged sword. At its best, the telephone is the adjuster's aid. It can slice through red tape, expedite claims-handling and enhance clear communication. At its worst, however, the phone produces unwelcome and irritating interruptions, becoming a downright obstacle to getting work done.

Too often, the telephone controls the adjuster, when just the opposite should occur. Adjusters should be the masters of, not slaves to, the telephone. Many adjusters, however, spend their entire workdays responding to bells, rings and noises — like dogs in some Pavlovian experiment. Admittedly, taming the telephone is easier said than done. We must acquire new habits and discard old ones.

(If you'll excuse me, I just got a phone call . . .)

Now, where was I?

For those seeking to master the telephone, let us first view some pitfalls to avoid. Here are some common approaches — often unsuccessful — to managing the telephone.

Brother, can you paradigm? Let's examine three ineffective paradigms of phone management.

The "Off-the-Hooker"

While avoidance may be a recognized approach of risk management, it is unacceptable in handling phone calls. Running from the problem is the "solution" for the off-the-hooker. By keeping the phone off the receiver, phone distractions are halted, or such is the theory. Perhaps the receiver is placed on the desk, hid in a drawer, or dangling on the floor. One charade employed by this character involves putting one's ear to the receiver as if one is on hold, when there is nothing more than a dial tone or busy signal on the other end of the line. Anyone trying to get a call through gets a perpetual busy signal.

Since there is no way to physically prevent people from calling, the off-the-hooker attacks the symptom of the problem. As callers phone in, off-the-hookers say, in effect, "You can't catch me!" Many have merely reached the end of their psychological rope in seeking ways to manage their volume of incoming calls. Keeping the phone off the receiver can be a seductive idea, a last-ditch effort to attain some serenity in order to accomplish work.

So professionally unacceptable, however, is the practice that those who covertly go off-the-hook often get called on the carpet. Let's face it, it's the coward's way. As the saying goes, "You can run but you can't hide!" Keeping the phone off the receiver is so repugnant that, with good cause, it invites managerial wrath. Deep down, the off the hooker knows this, hence his desire to make the process sub rosa.

Invariably, however, the off-the-hooker reaches the end of his predictably brief life-span. The habit is destined for discovery, and the aftermath will be most unpleasant.

Like the proverbial Dutch Boy with his finger in the dike, the off-the-hooker does nothing but postpone the inevitable and make its effect much worse. The Dutch Boy does not see the water level rising behind the dam. Nor does the water disappear just because a leak is temporarily plugged. The *source* of the problem remains unaddressed, only its effects are veiled from one's view. Once the water accumulates and cascades over the top of the dam, the situation rages out of control.

Off-the-hookers can no more control the telephone that the Dutch Boy can stem a rising tide. They address the effects and ignore the causes of their deeper problems. Both invite being overwhelmed by the long-term chaos their stopgap measures produce.

Don't Strike Out

Some adjusters think, "three strikes and they're out." These adjusters do nothing so drastic as prevent in-coming calls. No "jamming" tactics are used. Instead, this adjuster will not return any phone call until the caller has already phoned twice and has left two messages. On the third message, the adjuster finally returns the call. This adjuster throws down an obstacle course which each caller must run to speak with the intended target. This adjuster subjects callers to a Darwinian struggle where only the strong — and persistent — survive! (Translate: only the important calls will get through.)

Why the elaborate hide-and-seek game? The "three strikes" adjuster may be unconcerned with the reasons, but she assumes that if a call is *really* important, then the caller will be persistent enough to call and call and call. A "three strikes" adjuster can be overheard making remarks such as, "I never return phone calls until the third message." Generally, these remarks are made out of management's earshot. Bosses look unkindly on this winnowing process, especially since they often end up having to smooth the ruffled feathers of the angry people who have fought their way through.

Let's face it, adjusters absorb lots of nastiness and downright psychological abuse. They may thus be tempted to avoid friction altogether and take the path of least resistance. The "three strikes" approach is tempting for this reason. Its development, like the off-the-hook technique, must be secretive. One cannot use the "three-strikes" approach and serve clients. It betrays an arrogance toward the public and is the type of behavior that gives the insurance industry a bad name. Because of this, managers and supervisors do not tolerate the practice, if they are aware of it.

Eventually, though, the three-striker is called "out." The odds are simply against the tactic's success. Sometime a client will make that second or third call — not to Mr. Off-the-Hook — but to his boss, whose wrath will soon follow. Or, phone call number two may go to a competitor. An irate claimant may call a lawyer or the state insurance commissioner. An ignored first call may only trigger a blistering complaint, which is a reminder of the "three-striker's" haughtiness.

"Three strikes and I call" carries within it the seeds of its own downfall. Marginal unpleasantness dodged today invites larger problems later on. The "three striker" does not avoid unpleasantness by erecting an obstacle course for prospective callers. He merely postpones the grief, ensuring that it will likely reappear in a much more virulent form. The piper must, and will, be paid.

Mr. and Ms. Accessibility

Mr. or Ms. Accessibility does not avoid the telephone. Rather, he or she goes to the opposite extreme of the off-the-hooker. Accessibility Inc. prides themselves on the fact that they are indiscriminately available at any time for all calls, ranging from the trivial to the crucial. Self-importance is enhanced by the feeling that one is always in demand, constantly on the phone. Holding calls is an anathema, a sign of weakness. Blood rushes faster through Mr. Accessibility's veins as he mans the phone lines, fielding one call after another. Oh, how exhilarating!

How can one spot Ms. Accessibility? She is one who seems to have a telephone receiver surgically grafted to her ear. Sometimes Mr. Accessibility may even try to field *two* calls at once, if as many receivers are available. Each day offers another nonstop virtuoso performance. Accessibility Inc. sits down before the telephone as Vladimir Horowitz sits before a Steinway grand piano. How gratifying to know that one is so important, keeping one's fingers on the pulse of the claims world!

51

She also works very late. She has to, in order to accomplish the work that would have been done but for the phone call juggling act. In fact, she works late so often, she's on a first-name basis with the cleaning crew. If she does not work late, the job does not get done. As one relishes the challenge of seeing how many incoming calls can be fielded, one's job effectiveness becomes increasingly "phoney."

Passivity lies at the heart of Mr. Accessibility. He may fashion himself as a type of hard-driving fire fighter, but Mr. Accessibility spends most of his time *reacting* when he should be *acting*. Moving from phone call to phone call, his work day becomes an incoherent mess. Mr. Accessibility is not in control, he is the one who is controlled. He is so busy perpetuating the myth of his own indispensability that he emphasizes fire-fighting over crisis prevention. Being available at all times for all calls, having no screening system or way to prioritize, Mr. Accessibility tries to take the bull by the horns, but is likely to be gored nevertheless.

Vital work which the adjuster cannot perform within Ma Bell's ringing gets short shrift from Mr. Accessibility. This creates a different source of pressure from unhappy supervisors, managers, insurers and clients. Mr. Accessibility boosts vanity more than productivity.

Mired in the quicksand of phone call after phone call, the Accessibility Person cannot "work smart" or productively.

Now let's explore some specific tips on how the telephone can work *for* instead of against the insurance professional:

Tip #1: Self-Appraise Phone Use

You may think you have a good idea of who calls you most frequently, and what types of calls are the biggest drain on your time. Memories are subjective and notoriously unreliable, however, and a first step toward managing your telephone time is to systematically see how you spend your phone time. Track this!

For one week, log your incoming calls, both as to frequency, origin, and time of day. Alternately, save phone message slips from one week and then review them. Do certain callers predominate? Are there recurring requests? Are certain times of day or days of the week peak periods for incoming calls? Consider composing a pie chart, graphically depicting the sources of your calls. This helps you diagnose the way you spend your phone time and various sources of interruptions which might be curbed.

Tip #2: Return Phone Calls

How simple yet unheeded is this advice! Avoid later interruptions by promptly returning phone calls. This preempts a later, second phone call being made to you. It puts you in control of your time. Not to overlook the obvious, but good business and common courtesy also mandates this habit.

Ignored callers tend to call again. Believing otherwise is just wishful thinking. Do not neglect phone messages because "that guy is an S.O.B." or "I know what he's going to ask and I don't have an answer," or "I don't have settlement authority." Returning a phone call now squelches interruptions you might otherwise have later. In the long run, returning these calls *saves* time. You also avert the aggravation and embarrassment of having a persistent caller wind up complaining to your boss, the client, the Insurance Commissioner or an attorney!

If you can't call back immediately — either due to some crisis, travel vacation, illness, etc., have someone back at the office phone or even fax callers to let them know that you're indisposed and when they can reasonably expect to hear back from you.

If there is a person you absolutely dread calling — an irate claimant, an abusive attorney, an abrasive client — consider having a co-worker place the call and then hand the receiver to you. This may help you overcome the mental block of phoning, thereby curbing telephone procrastination.

Tip #3: Prioritize Return Phone Calls

While all phone messages warrant the courtesy of a reply, all phone messages are not created equal. Odds are that, upon returning to your office, you will receive a stack of phone messages. For example:

- Flaherty of Flaherty & Donaldson 688-2195
  Re: settlement of the Cassey case; demand is $10,000
- Bruno of Supplemental Auto Body 967-7776
  Re: paint job of quarter-panel, White's van
- Mr. Donahue/ACME Underwriters 888-1212
  Wants to schedule a meeting to discuss all open claims

Array these in terms of priorities and return the most important calls first. Examples: a message from an important client before the one from the claimant's attorney; the one from a large self-insured account before the message from the body shop.

Do not necessarily answer these messages in the same sequence in which they arrived. Some calls have a higher priority, and you should address these first. Conduct some form of triage, in arraying calls from most important, to moderately important, and so forth, right down the line.

Tip #4: Schedule Outgoing Calls

Think before phoning. Time your outgoing calls for a certain period of the day. Save phone messages, cluster them together and return them at one time during the day. During this time, knock out all your phone messages. This is more efficient that trying to answer them piecemeal, as they are handed to you. If this cannot always be done, it should still be your goal. By scheduling outgoing calls for, say, a few hours in the afternoon, you avoid later interruptions, preempt a later distracting phone call, and empower yourself to be more in control of the conversation.

Biorhythms are individualized. You probably know if you're a morning person or evening person. Certain periods of the day are better for you than others in terms of your alertness, energy level and patience. If returning calls is a tough task for you, schedule your outgoing calls during one of your "up" periods.

Avoid simply returning phone calls by habit, without any forethought. When you arrive at the office after being on the road or out for lunch, you will likely see a pile of phone messages. The temptation may be to drop everything and start right in on returning calls. By all means scan the messages. Some may be so critical that you must return them immediately. Try to defer others until later that same day, though, when you can concentrate on out-going calls. Prioritize!

Tip #5: Calibrate Calls to The Receiver's Schedule

Call people when they are most likely to be available. This sounds obvious, but is often overlooked. Professionals are likely to be in their offices and available at certain times.

Guide to Best Phoning Times

Attorneys	11 a.m.-2 p.m.; 4-5 p.m.
Bankers	Before 10 a.m.; after 3 p.m.
Business Owners	Between 10:30 a.m. and 3 p.m.
Clergy	Between Tuesday and Friday
Contractors	Before 9 a.m.; after 5 p.m.
Dentists	Between 8:30 and 9:30 a.m.
Doctors	Before 9:30 a.m.; after 4:30 p.m.
Engineers	Between 4 and 5 p.m.
Executives	After 10:30 a.m.
Homemakers	Midmorning and mid-afternoon
Manufacturers	Between 10:30 a.m. and 3 p.m.
Pharmacists	Between 1 and 3 p.m.
Retailers	Between 1 and 3 p.m.
Sales Managers	Afternoon
Salespersons	Weekends and rainy days
Teachers	Weekdays after 4:30 p.m.

Avoid phoning anyone during an obvious dinner hour. This may be convenient for you if you're working late in the office, but often guarantees you a hostile response. Just consider how *you* feel when pesky telemarketers interrupt you while you are trying to sit down to dinner.

One recent TV commercial shows a harried businessman talking into a phone receiver, "No, no, no. I'm returning the call that he returned after I called..." Avoid playing telephone tag. Think before phoning and call when the odds are in your favor.

Tip #6: Use Your "While You Were Out" Slips
Make notes on these slips. If you are returning a phone call and do not have your file handy, make notes on the conversation on

the "While You Were Out" slip. If the person whose call you are returning is unavailable, leave a message and note that on the slip. Record the date and time you called. This helps if there's ever a question about who is or is not returning calls, or if you simply forget whose calls you have returned. It saves time you otherwise spend by returning the same call twice.

Later, when you find the file, transcribe the note or clip it in the file. Buy a needle-type spindle or some type of clip for your desk so you can keep phone messages in one place. This keeps them from getting accidentally swept off the desk onto the floor, in the trash, stuck in the wrong file, etc. Using these slips for notations helps to knock out return phone calls, avoiding the need to intersperse your efforts with a "file hunt." Phone now — hunt later!

An alternative: make notes on "Post-It" slips, available at office supply stores. These adhesive slips stick to paper but will not damage it when pulled off. While talking on the phone, if you do not have your file at hand, write on a Post-It and stick that on you desk, or someplace prominent where it will be remembered. Later, match the note to the file and place it in the file. The Post-It notes come in a variety of sizes, the largest being about 4-by-6 inch.

Just make sure your desk does not begin to look like Post-It confetti was sprinkled over the top!

Tip #7: Confirm Appointments in Advance

Broken appointments can be huge time-wasters, but often they can be prevented simply by calling ahead a hour or so before you're scheduled to meet. This is one of many ways the telephone can be a tremendous time-*saver.*

Moral: Phone ahead just before you leave your office to make an appointment. For example, if an insured is supposed to meet you in your office, phone an hour or two in advance to confirm the appointment and to make sure it hasn't somehow slipped their mind. Damage estimators should make sure before they leave their office that the car will be at the body shop or at the claimant's home. Some people are fickle and forgetful. Others, especially witnesses who "don't want to get involved," are notoriously hard to pin down. A quick phone call just before leaving the office may avoid the frustration and wasted time of a broken appointment.

Tip #8: Use "On Hold" Time

Do you ever feel you spend much of your life "on hold"? Put this time to use! Examples of what you can accomplish during these scraps of time: refiling files, completing expense account forms, signing and proofreading letters, setting within reach the next file you will need. Any type of waiting time is a "scrap" which can be used for getting things done.

Tip #9: Hang Up and Dial Again

Do not hold indefinitely. Some claim professionals have a rule of thumb: if they're on hold for more than three minutes, they hang up and re-dial. Maybe the receptionist forgot about them. When receptionists ask, "Could you please hold?" answer, "For a minute, if you promise to check back with me." This may prevent you being placed in "limbo" land, completely forgotten while you hold the receiver to your ear. Keep some material on hand that you can work on to put this time to good use. Sitting and listening to Muzak is not the best use of time while on-hold.

Make sure that you get a phone with an "automatic re-dial button!

Tip #10: Just Say "No" When Asked to be Put on Hold

Do you receive calls which begin, "Please hold for..."? As more people have secretaries place outgoing calls, the practice seems to be growing. Some on the receiving end find it rude and resent this type of call. I have known some claims people who "just say no" and figure "if Mr. Important Busy wants to talk with him, he can call me."

Tip #11: Use "Hands-Free" Calling and Listening Technology

Newer phone systems enable you to camp on hold without having to cradle the phone receiver to your ear. Try to get this feature on your phone system. When you are put on hold, you can punch a "mike" (as in microphone) or speaker button and will hear when the person on the other end picks up. In the meantime, your hands are free for other tasks. You can also dial without having to pick up the receiver until the other party answers.

The Ploy's the Thing: How to Get Calls Returned

Failure to get calls returned is a common adjuster lament. Here are some specific ploys and tactics for dealing with this time-wasting and stomach-acid-producing problem.

Tip #12: Schedule a Phone Appointment

Use tactics which maximize your odds of having phone calls returned. How many times have you heard adjusters complain, "I can't get hold of..." or "He never returns my phone calls"? If, for instance, you're having a hard time getting lawyers or doctors to return your calls, ask their secretaries if you can schedule an *appointment*. At this juncture, confronted with the prospect of a face-to-face encounter, the elusive target may somehow manage to call to see what you have in mind. If he is so busy, then he may do whatever he can to avoid yet another meeting. Especially if he has been ignoring your messages, he may feel sheepish about an in-person meeting.

Tip #13: Grease the Wheels by Charming Receptionists

Get to know the staff of the people with whom you are dealing, especially secretaries and receptionists. Be friendly without being forward or presumptuous. Learn their names. A receptionist or secretary has ways of raising some messages to the top of the stack and calling them to the boss' attention. This may speed a return call.

Tip #14: Don't Accept "He's not in."

If you call and are told, "He's not in..." always ask if he is expected in later. Around what time? Is he expected back today? Amazingly, some receptionists will not *volunteer* that Ms. X is on vacation for two weeks or in a lengthy trial. As a result, you waste a lot of time spinning wheels trying to reach them daily by phone.

Tip #15: Give the Returnee a Breather Before Calling

If you know someone has been on vacation or out of the office for a while, don't call first thing on the Monday morning when he or she is back. Chances are they will be so swamped with accumulated work that they'll have little time to return your call or will be tool occupied to give you their undivided attention. Wait until later in the week. You'll be more likely to receive a call-back and the person on the other end will appreciate you giving them a chance to be back a few days and to catch up on accumulated work.

Tip #16: Go Around the Elusive Target

Instead of going over the head of the person you're trying to reach, consider someone else in that organization that you do know. In speaking with that person, casually mention that you are having a hard time getting through to "X," so he must be very busy. Your friend or acquaintance may mention this to "X," who now stands a much better chance of returning your call.

Tip #17: Establish a "Quiet-Hour" Within the Claims Office

A thin line separates this practice from becoming an off-the-hooker, so I mention this only reluctantly. Nevertheless, establishing a "quiet hour" by allowing no incoming calls for, say, an hour or two can often increase one's productivity many times over. Michigan Millers Insurance Company establishes a daily "quiet hour." Information and sensory overload is such a problem among businesses that some are taking matters into their own hands. Not all of these examples are from the insurance claim area, but they contain ideas which might take root and germinate there.

For example, a small group of Xerox software developers in Webster, N.Y. are experimenting with a "quiet hour," when they can't interact with others inside or outside the company. At Computer Associates (CA) in Islandia, N.Y., CEO Charles Wang limits e-mail access. CA employees read and send e-mail *only* before 9:30 a.m., at lunch or after 4:30 p.m. ("Surviving Information Overload," by Rick Tetzeli, *Fortune,* July 11, 1994, p. 65.) How often have you heard adjusters say that one hour of work before 9 a.m. or after 5 p.m. is worth two or three hours during normal business time? The reason: during quieter hours, the adjuster is free from the phone and can work uninterrupted.

Tip #18: Block Out Time for a Dictation Hour

Reserve dictation time for relatively quiet hours: prior to the start of the business day, during a working lunch, after 5 p.m. or during some time you carve out for yourself. Unhindered by phone interruptions, you can plow through dictation which originally you thought would take hours to complete.

Tip #19: Consider Selective Jamming

A partner with Baker & McKenzie, the world's largest law firm, once told me that his favorite button on his touch-tone phone was labelled "MSB." The initials stood for "make signal busy" and he could program it at will to deflect phone distractions. (And all the while, I thought the initials stood for, "Make Stupendous Bills"!) Newer phone systems often come with "DND" ("Do not disturb") buttons. These measures may seem extreme, but the point is that there may be times when you need to be freed of taking phone calls. Just don't abuse the practice!

Tip #20: Funnel Calls to Predetermined Hours

Another option: include on your business card the hours you are be available to accept phone calls. This doesn't mean you won't accept any calls outside of this time span, but it may influence people to call you only during certain times of the day. With some margin for error, you can channel calls to certain times of the day. Give these cards to claimants and claimant attorneys. I would not recommend them for clients, though. Consider printing two sets of business cards. One set — for clients — has your office number with no hours listed. The other set designates a specific telephone time-span. Indicating on your business card the hours you accept calls may create some "quiet time" and help you consolidate calls.

Tip #21: Schedule Interruption-Free Time for Yourself

If you're opposed to having calls held, consider other options. Instruct the receptionist or switchboard operator to tell callers that you are "in a meeting" or "in conference" (even if it means you are conferring with yourself!).

If you are worried about missing crucial calls, give the operator a list of V.I.P.'s, people to put through to you no matter what. Examples: a key client, your boss or spouse.

If the phone tends to drive you crazy, lower the volume on your phone as low as you can get it. This way the phone won't jangle your nerves (and eardrums) as much each time it rings. Must we be like Pavlov's dogs, responding to bells all day?

Tip #22: Let it Ring!

Or, just let the phone ring ... and ring. Don't answer. Maybe the receptionist will simply take a message, which you can return later in the day. Make sure this technique has your boss' sanction, though. In some offices, the receptionist will simply call you over an intercom-type pager. Hiding in the restroom stall is a short-term solution, until they string intercom wire into the lavatory!

Tip #23: Swap Phone Duty

Swap time with a colleague during which time you "cover" each others calls. This can be for a one or two hour span. Do this daily or assign a different day of the week for each person. This gives people a span of down-time, during which they can catch up on paperwork or attend to whatever projects tolerate no interruption.

Co-workers covering for another should be more than glorified receptionists. "I will have Mrs. Smith call you back after 2:00 p.m." is a lame response to incoming calls. Receptionists can do that! Instead, the "covering" person should be familiar with claims and, if not familiar with the particular file, they should have access to the files of the "covered" person. Importantly, they should be willing to answer questions and resolve the problems of in-coming callers. Otherwise, the "covered" person merely has to make that many extra return phone calls when their quiet period is over.

Make sure this policy has your boss' consent and make sure the receptionist knows to whom calls go through. Receptionists in most claim offices are harried and besieged by phone calls. It's hard enough remembering what calls and messages go where, much less diverting Jim's calls to Dave every Tuesday from 10 a.m. until noon. Be tolerant, patient and expect some "slippage" here.

Tip #24: Use Gadgetry to Your Advantage

Many gadgets are available which can make the telephone more of a time-saver than a time waster. Some of the time-saving gadgetry might include:

• Shoulder-cradles for the telephone receiver are useful for anyone spending much time on the phone, and allow hands-free calling.

- A touch-tone phone versus a rotary dial is another example. Cost factors are sometimes used as a reason to reject this idea. In the long run, however, time saved can outweigh any marginal cost increase. Increasingly, professional offices are moving to the touch-tone phone. (The author recalls his first claims manager, a member of the old guard who viewed modern inventions with old-fashioned skepticism. In the late 1970's and early 1980's he declined to install touch-tone phones for the adjusters on the basis that they cost too much!)
- phone head-set
- redial features
- speed dial options
- speaker phone

Tip #25: Speed Dial

Get a phone with a speed dial option. Many phone systems on the market enable the user to store frequently-used numbers in the phone's memory. Many systems allow users to program scads of frequently-called numbers: attorneys — both claimant and defense, clients, the home office, body shops, contractors, local hospitals, police stations, rental car firms, rehab outfits, surveillance firms, smoke and water damage restoration firms, workers' comp commissions, local hospitals and physicians, etc. Speed dial features let you hit one or two numbers and, presto, you are connected! Speed dialing can be used with local or long distance calls. Over the long run, less time spent dialing provides more time in other areas.

Tip #26: Get a Speaker Phone

Invest in a phone microphone box, or any device such as a custom "shoulder caddie" which frees you or your hands during phone discussions. This allows you to do more than just one task at a time: routing reports, searching for files, jotting down notes, etc. A caveat: "squawk boxes" may be inappropriate for important settlement negotiations or discussions with key clients. Voice quality in transmission varies greatly. You cannot make a good impression if your voice sounds like you're transmitting from a diving bell a hundred feet below the ocean!

Alternatives are available if you dislike the sound quality or lack of privacy that comes with a "squawk box." Consider a lightweight telephone head set similar to that used by operators. If you much time on the phone (and what adjuster doesn't?) consider using one of these for hands-free telephone work. You may get some funny looks from co-workers, but then, hey, why be a slave to fashion? Maybe you'll start a new trend!

Tip #27: Leave Precise Messages

Avoid "telephone tag" by leaving a precise message or instruction. Relay the message and say that the other person only has to call back if he has a question or wants to discuss. This saves time in answering return calls and avoid telephone tag. Be sure you make accurate file notes and documentation.

Do **not** use this technique for settlement discussions, but rather for less critical exchanges of information. Adjusters have faced potential errors-and-omissions claims because they made a settlement offer by way of a message which later became a matter of dispute. If you receive settlement authority or an offer via phone message, always follow up to confirm it by phone *and by letter* to avoid any later misunderstanding or recriminations about the accuracy of the figures relayed. A modern Confucius might say: "Use voice mail but create a paper trail."

Insurance consultant Dr. Ronald Anderson notes, "The message taking and delivering point is critical, because many errors and omissions claims develop from a breakdown in message taking or delivery."[1]

Tip #28: Organize Your Phone Numbers

Invest in a small phone directory or Rolodex and use it to list frequently-called numbers. Time spent here will pay dividends later. Sit down with a pen, your directory and the phone book. Think of *all* the people you call: doctors, lawyers, police stations, hospitals, clients, body shops, contractors, detective agencies, rehabilitation specialists, engineer consultants, court dockets, arbitration panels, carry-out pizza delivery, other insurance carriers, brokers, etc. Add and delete numbers as time passes.

This saves much time later, time which would otherwise have been frittered away paging through some phone book or folder. Put as many of these numbers as you can on speed dial! There are even Rolodex software programs where you can keep your phone lists on your PC — desk-top or laptop. Or personal organizers such as Casio's BOSS can help you carry around a portable Rolodex.

Tip #29: Use Conference Calls

Does this sound familiar?

Defense attorney Michaels calls you and explains the need to settle a bad products liability case for $400,000. He needs authority by next Monday. You do not have the authority, so you'll have to call your home office examiner and review all the points defense counsel has mentioned. Then, you'll have to call attorney Michaels to either grant authority or explain why it's not forthcoming. Maybe a co-defendant should contribute. Let's place a call to the representative of Northern Mutual. Another phone call. And so on and so on.

Instead of making all of these calls, use conference calls where you can get a lot of people on the line at one time. This way you'll avoid a lot of multiple phone calls up and down the line which consume a lot of your time. Your local phone service can offer instruction on conference call dialing, both local and long-distance.

Tip #30: Get to the Point!

Make sure that YOU — yes, you! — are not a windbag yourself. Telephone talk is not cheap (unless it's your lawyer doing the talking!). A recent national survey reveals that on average, executives spend fourteen (14) work weeks a year on business phone calls, much of it wasted time. Executives in this survey stated that they spend 2.3 hours each day on the phone. This equals 11.5 hours per week, or fourteen 40-hour weeks per year. Respondents also reported that 21 percent of their calls were wasteful or unnecessary — equal to three 40-hour work weeks per year. If this is true of executives, imagine what the figures might be for claim professionals, who seem to rely even more heavily on the telephone!

Before you phone, prepare an agenda of topics to be discussed. This helps avoid meandering conversations. Be friendly but businesslike. Set the tone:

Try...

"Jim, I've got a couple of items I need to discuss with you ..."

Instead of ...

> *"Hey Jim, Bruce. How's the weather there in Bangor? ... Really! How are the wife and kids?"*

When people call you, exchange pleasantries, then ask, "What's up?" This is a good way of getting to the point and getting meandering conversations on track.

Avoid open-ended questions which invite a meandering response or social chit-chat. Think about what you want to accomplish with each phone call. Minutes of preparation save hours in execution. Have a specific objective in mind when placing the call.

Handle Wind-Bags Deftly

Have you ever received calls from lawyers or claimants who talked as though the only thing they had to do in their lives was to talk to you about their claim? Some people just seem to find it therapeutic to unload on the claims adjuster. It's as though they hope to wear you down to their viewpoint by sheer stubbornness. These callers can be terrible time-wasters. How do you handle callers who have diarrhea of the mouth without losing control of the claim or appearing unprofessional?

Minimize long-winded and pointless telephone discussions. While this is tough, brevity needs to be tempered with courtesy.

Tip #31: Try the White Lie

Time management consultant Robert Moskowitz recommends telling the caller that you appreciate how busy *he* is, setting a timer, and later making up a "white lie" as to why you must get off the phone. A small timer at your desk or in a drawer helps remind you when phone conversations have run on too long.

Tip #32: Just Say No

Another option is simply to say "no" to those who want to buy, beg or borrow your time against your will. Most mistakes in life are created by saying "yes" too early or "no" too late!

Tip #33: Try, "Hello, I must be going..."

Another tactic is to tell the caller at an appropriate point, "I've got another call (or other calls) coming in..."

This will normally prompt them to sign off. Or, you can say "I was just on my way out the door when you called, what can I do for you?" This conveys the message that you don't have all the time in the world. Or, you can mention, "I was just in the middle of something when you called..." Alternately, ask them if you can call them back later **and do so.** Some people have been known to hang up on *themselves* in mid-sentence! Use these ploys long enough with windbags and maybe they'll get the point: either they'll call less often or they'll communicate with you by letter.

Tip #34: Keep a Mental List of Windbags

Keep a mental list of "chatterers." Every adjuster knows there are certain claimants, claimant lawyers, defense attorneys and even clients that are long-winded. If possible, communicate with these people by memo.

Tip #35: Time Your Return Calls to Minimize Windbaggery

Another technique: call them just before lunch or just before the end of the work day. This will help bring them to the point. If the caller is a notorious windbag, call back when you know he won't be available. That way you can't be accused of ignoring phone messages but you avoid having your time wasted by a chatterer. Telephone tag can sometimes work to your advantage!

Tip #36: Make a WRITTEN List of Windbags

Consider making more than just a mental list of chatterers. Write their names down, give them to a receptionist and ask her to take messages when these people call. Make sure your office policy condones this. Do not use this to avoid people you simply do not want to face. (PS: Make the list top-secret and tell the secretary not to release it to anybody, under penalty of death!)

(P.P.S.: Make sure that YOU'RE not a windbag with others!)

Tip #37: Use Voice Mail Effectively

"Hello. You have reached the voice-mail portion of this
  Chapter."
"If you'd like to fast-forward to another chapter, press 1,
  then pound sand."

"If you'd prefer to read the newest John Grisham novel, press 2."

"If you'd like to strangle your adjuster, press 3."

"If you'd like to do the hokey-pokey, press 4."

"If you'd like to blow this voice mail system to smithereens, press 0 or stay on the line."

You get the message.

Many claim offices — both for insurance companies and independent adjusters — use voice mail. Even if your own office lacks a voice mail system, you probably transact much business using voice mail. As companies reduce the personnel cost of full-time receptionists, this trend is likely to increase, not diminish. Today's claim professional must get used to voice mail and learn how to extract the most from it as an effective communication tool.

Voice mail can help or hinder effective claims communication, however. Voice may can be abused by claim reps if they use it for any of the following purposes:

- To shield claim reps from callers they wish to avoid;
- To serve as a personal secretary, never allowing anyone to get through directly (Perpetual voice mail is only one small step above taking the telephone off the receiver.); or
- To insulate claim reps from clients and customers. Claim work often loses its personal touch with voice mail because transactions occur between recorded voices over the phone — "I'll have my machine call your machine ..."

Voice mail often evokes frustrations in users who are calling in to receive claim service. Multiple commands and convoluted instructions can make voice mail tough for users to follow. Some callers may be irked because they already know what — or who — they want, but are powerless to fast-forward through the maze of recorded instructions. (Tip to offices installing voice mail: incorporate an option for callers who want to immediately connect with a real live, breathing human being!) Also, incorporate a feature where schooled callers can fast-forward without having to listen to the recording for the 1,538th time.

Other callers get frustrated when they navigate the voice mail maze, finally reach a human being, only to be placed on hold because the claim reps are "busy." On some voice mail systems, hitting zero on the Touch-Tone telephone connects callers to a receptionist or switchboard operator, who can answer questions and alleviate voice-mail frustration.

For all of its imperfections, though, voice mail has significant benefits in managing time, if used wisely.

- It helps avoid telephone tag. If a claim representative, for example, has a quick question or a very specific request, voice mail works well. For instance, a claims adjuster can leave a question on another person's voice mailbox. If the adjuster is unavailable when that person phones back, the caller can leave the answer on the adjuster's machine and short-circuit telephone tag. Voice mail is ill-suited, though, for lengthy discussions on more substantive matters. If it is necessary to discuss a topic or topics, or to brainstorm ideas, do not rely on voice mail.
- Voice mail is very flexible, allowing the claims professional to retrieve messages from anywhere at any time.
- Properly used, voice mail can actually improve client service. How? You can leave and receive messages twenty-four hours a day. There is no need to compose a letter or engage in meandering chit-chat.

Claim professionals with voice mail must discipline themselves to still return phone calls promptly. Answering machines and voice mail should not become crutches. All users should carefully balance quiet time in the office with a time period of open telephone lines. Certain callers and clients will balk at being herded into the voice-mail maze. Many of the complaints about voice mail are — when boiled down — really complaints about the *abuse* of voice mail rather than a convincing critique of the technology itself.

If you are a fan of voice mail and see its time-saving features, then urge your service providers to incorporate it into their operations. If you work, for example, with a law firm that has voice mail, ask for a directory of extensions. Lawyers, insurers, agencies, brokerage houses and many other businesses increasingly use voice mail and have extension directories.

Much benefit flows to the claims professional who becomes the master, rather than the servant, of the telephone. Interruptions otherwise intruding on productive time are squelched. Potential crises are defused at an early stage. More work can be done in less time. Adjusting should be a more rewarding and downright enjoyable job.

By taming the telephone, the claims professional can ensure that "reach out and touch someone" does not become the epitaph for continually unfinished business.

NOTES
1. Dr. Ronald Anderson, *Agents' Legal Responsibility*, National Underwriter Company, Cincinnati, 1980, p. 109.

Chapter Five

On The Road Again: Maximizing Out-of-Office Time

Adjusters spend much "bread and butter time" outside the office. With the advent of telephone adjusting, this may come as a surprise. Some claim professionals rarely venture from their offices to tackle the challenges posed by face-to-face claim investigations. Top-notch adjusters, however, have a common denominator: the desire to leave the office and hit the road to investigate. Daily, these adjusters get out of the office and out on the road. Far from being a way of escaping work, road trips are the primary modus operandi for quality investigators. While paperwork cannot be handled from behind the wheel of a car, claims cannot be investigated solely from the vantage point of one's desk chair.

If claim departments and, especially, independent adjusting offices are to survive and transcend tough economic times, they must excel in outside investigations. Many insurance companies refer cases to independent adjusters because the latter are supposedly *not* tied to desks. If a telephone-handled claim was all that a client needed, odds are it would not have referred out the case to begin with! Why would an insurer or self-insured pay for an independent adjuster to become a "telephone jockey"? Through personal contact, by gathering first-hand impressions of all aspects of a claim, the outside adjuster serves as the client's eyes and ears. By avoiding personal contact and clinging to the office like a security blanket, the outside adjuster is simply wimping out.

Despite internalizing claims-handling and a trend toward telephone adjusting, there will always be a need for the outside adjuster who budgets time wisely. High exposure cases — fatalities, explosions, major cargo losses — will always exist and require professionals who hit the road and get the job done. Hands-on expertise will replace telephone adjusting on serious claims. Repeatedly, the adjusters who stand out are those willing to hustle, to get out into the field, and who manage their time well. As it is with individuals, so it is with companies. Organizations committed to quality face-to-face claims handling will, in the long run, surpass those trying to get by with a slapped-together telephone job.

Despite the positive aspects of field work, many adjusters still avoid it. Why?

Insecurity may be one reason. For the adjuster unsure of his abilities, eye-balling a claimant may be uncomfortable. Using the telephone, the adjuster avoids the momentary discomfort created by face-to-face encounters. For this adjuster, keeping holed up in the office is one way to sanitize encounters and to keep hostile persons at bay. Often, a deep-seated insecurity makes adjusters cling to their offices.

Sheer laziness may prevent some adjusters from leaving their chairs and getting behind the wheel of their cars.

Adjusters may feel insecure about their jobs, and may feel that they have to be seen in the office a lot so that their supervisor, manager, etc. will know (or think) they are working. This adjuster fears that being out of the office may be seen as a work shortage on the adjuster's part, when just the opposite is the case. Visibility in the supervisor's eyes is the goal toward which this type of claimsperson strives. Such adjusters mistake visibility for effectiveness. They figure the best way to show everyone how hard they work is to have everyone see them, and the office best showcases their "busy-ness." For adjusters fond of highly structured work days, being out of the office may be synonymous with "goofing off."

Compulsive adjusters have difficulty blasting themselves out of the office because they cannot defend their turf. Like any other profession, claims adjusting probably has its share of "control freaks." This breed of adjuster strives to be totally in control, and often has a penchant — if not an obsession — for neatness. Blood pressure rises in this adjuster when she sees her desk groaning under incoming correspondence, outgoing reports, drafts to sign, new case assignments and the like. In the quest for a tidy desk, in the desire not to miss anything important while away, the compulsive adjuster takes the most direct solution: staying in the office, keeping antennae tuned, vigilant to defend turf. A territorial imperative develops and overcomes the need to leave the office to obtain positive results on files. A thin line separates being detail-oriented (a virtue) with being compulsively tidy (a vice). The adjuster who acquires the latter quality tends to stay planted firmly in the office.

We have all heard the phrase, "Out of sight, out of mind." Insecure claim-persons may fear that frequent absence from the office will be mistaken for laziness. Perhaps he fears being passed over for positions of greater responsibility, of being slighted in some way as a penalty for not hanging around the office, where the action is. They fear that absence will not make the boss' heart grow fonder.

Past a certain point, it is academic to explore further the psychological reasons for being terminally desk-bound. Understanding the trait does not exonerate the weakness or obscure its detrimental effects. Suffice it to say that some outside adjusters spend too much time inside the office and that time spent on the road is often poorly managed. In what ways can the claims professional manage his or her "outside" time more effectively?

Tip #1: Planning Pays Off

As in so many other aspects of claims handling, "Those who fail to plan, plan to fail." Minutes spent planning save hours in execution. A little planning can go far in making road trips more productive, earning the adjuster a greater return on the investment of out-of-office time. Planning road work involves more than simply knowing in advance where you are going to be on a particular afternoon. It is more than jotting down the time for an appointment on your desk diary for next week. And yes, it involves more than merely seeing to it that your Friday afternoon appointment is conveniently located five minutes away from your home. How can one plan to use out-of-office time most productively?

Tip #2: Consolidate Trips

Plan out-of-office trips by consolidating as much as possible. Never work on only one file per trip. This is a time-waster. Before leaving the office, study a map of the general area where you are headed. Ask yourself: is there anything else in this area or on another file which needs to be done? For instance, after photographing an accident scene, you might be able to catch that witness who lives nearby, or conduct an activity check while on your road trip. Do not randomly schedule outside appointments. Cluster tasks together. If you carefully plan road trips, you boost your productivity.

Tip #3: Avoid Dumb Cold Calls
   "Blind calls" or "cold calls" often turn out to be time-wasters. Much of this is due to the adjuster just not thinking or using common sense. If you must make a "blind call," do it when people are most likely to be home. Don't call on a businessperson's residence in the middle of the afternoon and expect to find him at home. Adjusters often overlook the common-sense approach. Why? Because often this time will be at a time most *in*convenient to an adjuster's personal schedule: evenings, weekends, etc.
   If your "target" is not home, leave your business card in the door.
   Before making a "cold call," grab some envelopes and office stationary. If you miss your intended person, write him a note telling him you need to talk with him and/or that you'll return at a different time. Slide the note in a envelope under the door or in the mailbox.
   Timing activity checks in the claimant's neighborhood can be a delicate matter. Visit only when you can realistically expect neighbors to be home. On the other hand, the person on whom you're checking may be home at this time too!
   Take along a camera. This practice served me well once while conducting an activity check in the neighborhood of a bodily injury claimant with a "bum knee." He had been walking across the grass in front of a church, when he stepped into a slight depression, allegedly injuring his knee. Naturally, he did what most of us would do in such a situation — he got a lawyer and threatened to sue the church! When I went to cold-call his neighborhood, I spotted the claimant climbing up and down a ladder, painting his house. I scrapped plans to query neighbors at that time and discreetly took snapshots of the claimant's exertions. Upon notify-

ing claimant's counsel of this, we leveraged a very modest settlement. (At that time, the claimant went from stepping into a depression to actually being in one.)

Moral: Observe the Boy Scout motto — "Be prepared" and take your camera!

Like a good real estate agent, you should get to know the neighborhood in advance. For example, before driving to the claimant's neighborhood, review the City Directory for the names and phone numbers of the folks who live nearby. When you knock on their doors, use their names. Neighbors will be more likely to open up to you and tell you about the claimant's activities if you know their names and project an air of command and competence. If you strike out and the neighbors are also gone, you can later phone them from your office and use their name. Obviously this is a touchy matter, and there is no guarantee of success. A few common-sense steps, however, can help ensure that activity checks will not be time wasted.

Tip #4: Think About Return Trips

Admittedly, often there is no substitute for the adjuster camping on the proverbial doorstep. As my first claims manager used to say, "They've gotta' come home sometime!" (It was such a mantra of his that the phrase became an inside joke among the adjusting staff.) If a witness is employed, don't call on his apartment in mid-morning. Such wheel-spinning only results in the adjuster reporting, "We made a blind call at John Jones' house but, unfortunately, no one was home." No wonder! If the first call misses pay-dirt, make sure the next attempt is on a different day, at a different time. Variety is not only the spice of life, but it is also a good way to improve your "hit ratio" on return trips. *Think* about it first!

Tip #5: Consolidate More

Many adjusters, especially those working in large cities, lament the great part of their lives which they spend stuck in traffic. "Hurry up and wait" becomes more than a phrase. Instead, it becomes the adjuster's daily observance. What claims-person has *not* at one time or another gotten caught in a traffic jam while commuting to work, leaving work, or heading for an appointment? Often, the adjuster's mind races with the thoughts of all that could be done were he not sitting in some line of backed-up traffic. Helplessness turns to frustration as the trapped adjuster wonders what he ever did to deserve wasting a great part of his life on the freeway. Commuter blues can often sabotage productivity and effective time management.

Plan for that down time! Carry a dictaphone with you while you travel, either by car or by air. Stuck on the Woodrow Wilson Bridge over the Potomac River for a few hot hours one summer afternoon, I was able to dictate a full formal captioned report on a premises liability claim. (Other commuters did a double-take, thinking I was crazy.) Memos and instructions to staff can be dictated. Prepared mailers are available in case you want to mail these cassettes back to your office. In this way you can delegate and manage while away from the office and reduce the paperwork you'll face when you return.

Consolidate more. Plan your appointments so that you hit the highways at non-peak, non-rush hours.

Tip #6: Map Out Local Travel

Invest in a good local road atlas. If you cover a large territory, you may need three or four map sets for different counties. (If your boss won't spring for them, buy them yourself and write them off on taxes as a business deduction.) Local car travel will be much more efficient if you map out your route in advance, preferably the day or night before. Paper-clip to your map a small card or slip of paper with step-by-step directions. Scan the map in advance. Do not try to wing it once you're on the road. Call your destination in advance and ask the folks there for directions. (You may learn a shortcut or find out problems to avoid: construction, one-way streets.) Take a high-lighter or pen and mark on your map frequently-travelled routes or locations.

Tip #7: Factor in Parking ... or Lack of It

Don't forget about parking! This can be a huge headache, especially in downtown areas. When calling ahead for directions ask them if nearby parking is available. Is there on-street parking, a parking lot for the office building, a parking garage, metered parking, reserved parking? Is parking a problem? Will you need quarters when all you have are bills or dimes? These niggling details may spell the difference between wasting time or being cool, calm and collected when you reach your destination. If so, allow yourself a time-cushion. Are spaces reserved? Nothing is as frustrating or time-wasting as getting to your destination on time but circling the block for twenty minutes hunting for a parking space. It is also an embarrassing time-waster to find a parking space only to find out the charge is $2 an hour and you didn't bring enough money. Factor in parking when planning driving trips.

Tip #8: Plan Smart to be "On Time"

Punctuality is important for claims professionals. Tardiness creates the wrong foundation for instilling trust with claimants, insureds or professionals. You must convey the impression of "split second" reliability. If you have a problem being on time for meetings and appointments, a few simple steps will help.

On your diary or calendar sheet, enter your **departure** time instead of the meeting/appointment time. Make sure you've backed out enough of a cushion to reach your destination, though.

Trick yourself into being on time by setting your watch or clock ten to fifteen minutes ahead. This will put you "back to the future" when it comes to making appointments on time.

Flying the Not-So-Friendly Skies

You don't have to be a registered "flying adjuster" to have an occasional need for air travel. Claims professionals occasionally travel by air (usually with the benefit of an airplane!). Their territory may be large. A catastrophe in a distant area may require their presence, a la a "Cat Team." They may have to call on clients or drum up new business in another area. Seminars, meetings and conventions require long-distance travel. Airline delays have prompted the modern advice: "If you're in a hurry, drive. If time is no object, fly."

Your job is to outwit the airlines, whose overall service is abysmally low and whose stratagems seem to be designed to frustrate your efforts at getting what you want. You can sit on the ground, number 34 for takeoff, and if the airlines pull away from the gate when they should, they will record that as "another on-time departure!" There is so much about air travel that the airlines, in their smiling chirpy TV ads, fail to disclose.

"Honey-roasted peanuts have become a symbol of passenger deprivation." — Bill Kizorek, President, InPhoto Surveillance and worldwide traveller

Let's bypass those peanuts for a moment and consider some ways to make air travel as time-efficient as possible.

For business travel by plane, a few considerations can save much time.

Tip #10: Get a Good Travel Agent

Cultivate a good working relationship with a local travel agent. The latter can book your flights, get you your preferred seat (e.g., window or aisle), special meal (e.g., kosher or vegetarian), make rental car and hotel arrangements. A travel agent can deliver your tickets and boarding passes in advance, saving you time at the terminal. If you belong to frequent flyer clubs, give the travel agent your membership number and often she can make sure you're automatically credited with the mileage. Use these for first-class upgrades or for free companion tickets. One benefit of first class is the extra room you get if you want to work in-flight.

Tip #11: Plan a Detailed Air-Travel Itinerary

Prepare an itinerary showing flight times, name of airlines, flight numbers, the locations of your meetings, fax and phone numbers where you can be reached. Also include the names of the folks that you will be meeting. Make four copies of this itinerary: one for yourself, one for your secretary, one for your spouse and one for your hotel. Distribute these to each a few days before your trip. This saves time in case something urgent arises while you're out of town.

Tip #12: Get There Early

Get to the airport at least an hour — or maybe even two — before departure. Avoid driving yourself to the airport but if you must, allow yourself enough time to park in a remote area and take a shuttle bus to the terminal. This is a greater consideration at large metropolitan airports, where the "satellite parking" may be miles away from the terminal. At some large airports, you must factor in:

- a traffic jam in getting to the airport
- time spent trying to find a parking space
- waiting at some forlorn outpost for a shuttle bus
- riding on the shuttle bus to get to the main terminal
- waiting in line to check luggage, buy tickets or get an upgrade
- taking a shuttle or rail from the main airline terminal to the mid-field terminal.

When returning home from a business trip, reverse the process. And those are just the *initial* delays. Factor in bad weather at the airport from which you are departing, bad weather at the airport where you're headed and you have further delays. Add in the possibility of some equipment or maintenance snafu, the pilot having a sniffle or the flight attendant clocking out because she's done her maximum shift and further delays can be in store.

Are you still sure that air travel is the fastest way?

The problem isn't flying — it's all the tedious time-wasting crap which passengers must endure just to get airborne.

Allowing a big cushion will help avoid missing flights.

Hope for the best but plan for the worst. Start from the premise that there will be delays and take enough reading and work along in order to fill this "down time."

Tip #13: Seek Direct, Non-Stop Flights

Always seek a non-stop direct flight. The more connections you have to make, the greater the odds that you'll be subjected to a delay. It is a little-known fact that not all direct flights are non-stop! The airlines have their own nomenclature and you might find yourself on a "direct flight" from Los Angeles to New York which stops in Denver.

Tip #14: Avoid the Hubs

Avoid major hub airports notorious for delays, such as Chicago's O'Hare or Atlanta's Hartsfield.

When you die and go to heaven, you have to change planes in Atlanta.

If you're planning to connect at a hub at "rush hour," don't be surprised if you're hung up with air traffic or weather delays. In fact, expect them. You are inviting delays if you connect through a hub at rush hour. If you land at New York's LaGuardia Airport between 7 a.m. to 9 a.m., expect to sit in traffic at least an hour and probably more, trying to fight your way into Manhattan. Try one of the so-called water shuttles, which bypass the sclerotic roads leading into New York City.

Tip #15: Monitor On-Time Records of Airlines

Certain airlines are also famous for flight delays and overbooking. Recent newspaper coverage has highlighted certain airlines (e.g. Continental) which lead the list of customer complaints to the Federal Aviation Administration. Keep this in mind when you book your flight or communicate your preferences to your travel agent.

Carry with you a pocket OAG, Official Airline Guide, in case you have to change a flight to get to your destination or back home. This gives you your choices of alternate flights if you are delayed, bumped or canceled on another flight.

Tip #16: Leave the Night Before

Poor airline service is driving some business travellers away from certain airlines and airports. (Some folks consider the phrase, "airline service" to be an oxymoron, sort of like "jumbo shrimp" or "military intelligence.") It is leading them to book flights at off-peak hours and to schedule trips so that they arrive the night before a morning meeting.[1]

If you have a morning meeting in another city, consider arriving the night before. Although the corporate bean-counters might instinctively balk, it might make financial sense. "Missing a business meeting is very costly," says Mitchell York, Editor of *Business Travel News*. "If you have an 11:00 a.m. meeting and you leave at 8:00 a.m. and miss the meeting because you don't arrive until early afternoon, it might cost $1 million, compared with $125 for a [hotel] room. It's opportunity cost, not just cost" that is critical, he says.[2] You may have to make this case to supervisors holding the purse strings, who increasingly study travel budgets with microscopic scrutiny. Flying off-peak hours the night before may also save your company money on air fare. You may be more rested and in a better frame of mind for conducting business as well.

Tip #17: Don't Check Your Bags

Why give the airlines one more opportunity to screw up and hold you up? Carry on your baggage instead of checking it. This saves you time that would otherwise be spent waiting at the baggage claim carousel. It also eliminates the chances that your bags will get lost, another tremendous time-waster, not to mention an un-nerving situation. If your bags get lost or mis-routed, much of the "penalty" is the time-wasting hassle of finding a bored baggage representative who — in between sweeping up — might be able to help you fill out forms, and tacking on about an hour's worth of delay. Even after all this, the airline will often be coy and non-committal about when, or whether, you will get your luggage.

The airlines whine about passengers carrying too much on board, overlooking the fact that if the airlines had a better record of not losing or mis-routing luggage, passengers would be less inclined to carry on. Give the airlines as few opportunities as possible to delay you — carry on your bags. You are in a battle of wits with the airlines. You've already paid for the flight, so you really don't have a lot of leverage.

One nice advantage of belonging to one of the flyer club's "elite" levels is that you get first-boarding privileges. This helps you in the never-ending competition for overhead bin space. Also, you get to seat yourself first and set up your work space. If the seat next to you remains unclaimed, you can spread out and have almost as much room as you would have had in first-class.

Tip #18: Get a Power Seat

Get an aisle seat. If you stow a briefcase or other materials overhead, they will be much more accessible here. (You also won't have to waste as much time crawling over passengers if you need to reach the lavatory in a hurry!) If possible, try to fit your briefcase underneath the seat in front of you. While it might give you less legroom, your work materials will be more accessible than they may be when squeezed in the overhead bin.

Tip #19: Plan Your In-Flight Time

Treat your air travel as a multi-hour span free of interruptions. Plan your in-flight time with a To-Do list. In flight you have a good chance to read, finish paperwork, and dictate. Forget the in-flight magazine. Go easy on the alcohol too: flying dehydrates you anyway and alcohol is a diuretic. You want to reach your destination feeling as physically strong as possible.

Tip #20: Keep Working After Touchdown

Don't stop working once the plane lands. Experience shows it may still be 10-15 minutes before the plane reaches its gate. Avoid the knee-jerk reaction of dropping everything the instant the plane touches down.

Tip #21: Join a Club

In addition to one of the high-mileage clubs for which you qualify after a certain number of miles, join at least one of the clubs — such as United's Red Carpet or American's Ambassador Club — which offer access to a lounge and business area at selected airports. These areas are often equipped with desks, fax machines, work spaces, phones, meeting rooms, photocopy machines, and other amenities which provide a civilized alternative to the holding pens provided by the airlines in their main gate areas. The quieter atmosphere is much more conducive for getting work done. If you're stuck in an airport, you can set up shop and conduct business from one of these lounges geared for the business traveller.

Tip #22: Reconsider Rental Cars

If you consider air travel an over-valued time-waster, think twice about renting a car as opposed to using taxi or limo service. Car rentals are often big time-wasters. Even with advance arrangements, you often must wait at the registration counter and then fill out paperwork. Then you get to walk to the pick-up area and wait for their shuttle. Once the shuttle drives you to your car you must stop at another booth while an attendant checks for more information. Dig your driver's license out of your wallet — AGAIN — and present the rental contract. The whole process can consume 45 minutes to an hour. Unfortunately, it's not as simple as just flying in and picking up your rental car as depicted in the car agencies' perky TV ads. If you must rent a car, try to get one with in-terminal service.

Be very careful and check out in advance the location of the car rental facility if it's an off-brand agency or one you have not used before. Some rental car companies advertise that they are "right on the airport." The unsuspecting might think that means *inside* the airport, but that is not the case. (What in the heck *does* it mean, anyway?) You might find that "right on the airport" means a fifteen-minute drive, with the rental car facility sandwiched in between Bruno's Body Shop and the Pink Slipper Dance Lounge. Is this worth the ten bucks price savings from going with an "off-brand" rental car company? Nothing is quite so frustrating as standing at the rental pickup area, waiting for the courtesy bus of the off-brand rental car company, while the Hertz and Avis vans have already made two pickup rotations. At this point, the marginal cost-savings is a false economy.

Needless to say, before you leave town you should call ahead and get explicit driving directions to each destination you're headed, along with estimated driving times. Read these back to the person giving them to you, to help assure accuracy.

Tip #23: Get a Phone Card

While on the road, you'll probably be phoning your office and receiving messages to call other people. Get a telephone charge card from one of the many long-distance services. This saves time scrambling around for change in airports or waiting for confirmation from your employer if you're charging the call to their number. It also provides a consolidated record of calls made while on business.

Tip #24: Keep a Bag Packed

If you do lots of air travel and some of it at the spur of the moment, have a bag packed and ready to go at all times, including clothes, toiletries, etc. Media magnate Ted Turner is said to do this so he can leave at a moment's notice.

Tip #25: Carry a "Portable Desk"

Importantly, take along enough paperwork and reading material so that if you are delayed (or even if you're on schedule) you can fill the time productively. Use your briefcase as a portable desk. Carry your laptop computer along. Take along some blank expense account forms and complete them during your trip. Your expenses will be fresher in your mind, you will save yourself some time once you return to the office and you may even get reimbursed quicker! There are also some special travel kits you can purchase which have miniaturized office supplies. I have one which easily carries a small version of: stapler, staple-remover, high-lighter, scissors, Exacto knife, ruler, staples, eraser, tape measure, scotch tape and tape dispenser, rubber bands and paper-clips. (Throw in a small calculator.) The entire pack zips up and weighs probably no more than eight ounces. This type of kit will save you time and aggravation while on the road. They are lightweight and consume very little space.

Tip #26: Knock-Out Paperwork on the Road

Take along a dictaphone and, on the return trip, dictate correspondence and reports generated by your travel. Your trip activities will be fresher in your mind at that point too. Consider this as part of the venture. You won't have these tasks hanging over you when you return to your desk, which is probably chock full of work that has sprouted during your absence!

Tip #27: Use Car Commuting Time Wisely

Can anyone beat life in the slow lane? Far from having to be a colossal waste of time and energy, however, commuting time can be turned to your advantage. Commuting time is usually put to no productive use, unless fuming, listening to top-forty hits or car dealership ads is your idea of effective time management. Time spent travelling and waiting is often overlooked as a useful source of productive opportunity.

Moral: Put commuting time to work for you. On New York's Long Island Expressway, for example, commuters stuck in traffic can be seen balancing checkbooks, doing crossword puzzles and dictating letters.[3] Driving to and from work, travelling to and from appointments can be used for purposes other than just radio-listening. Here are examples of how commuting time can be used more intelligently. While driving, you can:

- mentally review the important items needing to be done that day, or the next day;

- concentrate on what you want to accomplish from the upcoming meeting, statement, negotiating session, etc.;
- dictate a letter if you have your portable dictaphone with you;
- listen to a tape on an insurance course, or any self-improvement tape; or
- perform stress-relieving isometric exercises.

Thomas Jefferson did not have to face bumper-to-bumper traffic in his day — perhaps just horse-to-horse jams — but travel was still slow and tedious. His own approach to time management is instructive: "Determine never to be idle. No person will have occasion to complain of the want of time who never loses any ... It is wonderful how much may be done if we are always doing."

Put this block of time to use! Uses of commuting time are limited only by your imagination. While driving in your car, you are free of many distractions and interruptions which plague you back at the office: ringing telephones, uninvited guests, etc. Take advantage of the setting! Particularly in large cities and very desolate areas, commuting may be an untapped resource for "getting things done." Psychologist and self-improvement guru Denis Waitley calls his car his "university on wheels." View commuting as an opportunity, not an obstacle. In other words, turn a liability into an asset, a negative into a positive!

Tip #28: Move in Closer
When considering commuting, don't overlook the obvious. Your best time-management tool may lie in simply *moving in closer to your office*. A difference between 15 and 25 minutes commuting time each way may seem insignificant: it's only a ten-minute difference. Extrapolated over the course of the year, though, an adjuster driving 25 minutes each way will spend almost 87 hours in the car more than the other adjuster spending 15 minutes driving each way. That insubstantial ten minutes each way amounts to over *two work weeks* per year spent in the car! Moral: weigh the merits of moving in closer. Find a suitable habitat which is closer to your claim office!

Tip #29: Consider Public Transit or Car-Pooling
Consider using public transit instead of your car. On the bus or

subway, you can do work that you could never do — safely — in a car. Let someone else do the driving, or join a car pool where your attention can focus on matters other than driving. Get a portable cassette player and listen to the same tapes you would hear in your car if you were driving.

Tip #30: Use Waiting Time

Waiting time can also be deployed. You can bank these "pennies of time" and redeem them for "time dollars" later. For example, lawyers are notorious for having adjusters "cool their heels" in the reception area prior to an appointment. Whether a conscious psychological ploy or the byproduct of a genuinely heavy work schedule, the waiting game with plaintiff lawyers is a common experience for the claims professional. Nor is this the only venue where the Waiting Game is played. Standing in line at City Hall waiting for a copy of the Fire Marshal's report can drive you crazy, as you watch the slow-moving clerks who seem to be forever "on break."

Expect to wait and be prepared for it. Use this waiting time, though. One consultant suggests viewing waiting time as a "study hall." When people are late for appointments (as they often are), you often find yourself inside an office or outside someone's house. This too is a scrap or "penny of time" which you can productively use:

- Mentally review the important questions to ask if you are preparing to take a statement, for instance.
- Complete your expense account form.
- Review your schedule for that day, or the next.
- Take reading material along in your briefcase.
- Write or dictate a letter.
- Phone in to see if there are any important messages you can return while you have a little bit of time on your hands.

For those who treasure driving time as a period to decompress, these suggestions may seem too harsh. Admittedly, the approach requires self-discipline. It may not be the best technique for everyone. For those keenly interested in maximizing their productivity, though, commuting and waiting time can be deployed effectively. Rather than being irritating obstacles, these periods can be *oppor-*

tunities for effective time management. Turn a negative into a positive!

Tip #31: Get a Car Phone

Car phone prices are dropping like lead weights. If you log much time on the road or cover a wide geographic area, consider a car phone. Ask your company to spring for it. If they won't, then perhaps your employer will share the cost with you. Any portion of the cost you bear you might be able to write off on taxes as a business expense.

Advantages of having a car phone are clear. Your in-office time is spent more efficiently because you don't have to spend as much time returning phone calls — you've already returned them! Out-of-office time is turbo-boosted because you can do more than merely drive and listen to the radio. Nor do you have to waste time driving around, hunting for a pay phone so you can check in with your office. If you're stuck in traffic en route to an appointment, you can phone ahead and avoid ruffled feathers. Being more accessible to clients and quicker on the response has service advantages aside from improved efficiency.

If just one new business opportunity opens up for you due to a car phone, then this gadget will have paid for itself many times over.

Tip #32: Be a Minute-Man (or Woman)

Most work done outside the office is (or should be) planned. This is fundamental: through effective planning, you boost your productivity. Occasionally, however, we lack the luxury of planning field work. Often, adjusters are called out on very short notice to rush to an accident scene. Some clients use adjusters as an emergency room service, which is okay, but there is little time for planning and deliberation. "Mayday" calls run the gamut of tractor-trailer accidents, cargo turn-overs, bus collisions, storm losses, and the like. For offices whose clients include trucking lines, buses, car fleets and residential property, many "call-outs" will beckon claims service on the spur of the moment.

Adjusters often dread such calls, no matter how often they are reminded that these are simply part of the job which goes with being an outside adjuster. Call-outs are most likely to roust the adjuster from bed at 3:00 a.m. or pull him from the office near closing time on Friday afternoon, just before a three-day holiday weekend. Rare is the claims-person who likes dropping everything and attending to the crisis of the moment. Without enjoying the short notice call-out, there are ways to be prepared and to maximize effectiveness when duty calls.

Tip #33: You Can't Play the Game Without Proper Tools
"Be prepared" is a motto which works well for more than just the Boy Scouts. When it's your turn to have the duty, keep on hand certain essential items, whether they be in your office, at home or in your car:

- portable recorder *with recharger*
- telephone adaptor for taking recorded statements or information
- plenty of spare R/S cassettes
- R/S summary sheets with envelopes
- signed statement pad with extra sheets
- claim assignment sheets
- camera with flash, plenty of film and batteries
- tape measure
- notebook and pens

Other items easily forgotten but which are very helpful for on-the-scene investigations are:

- good map(s) of the locale
- a flashlight
- a full tank of gas
- money

I knew an adjuster who wasted two hours getting to a train derailment scene because he had to find an all-night drug store to buy camera film and a gas station for his car, which had a tank sitting on "E". Nothing may make a call-out enjoyable, but being prepared makes it a less onerous burden.

Tip #34: If it's not Your Turn ...
If you are phoned when you are not first on the list, **never** ask a client to call the person who is first on the recorded message. Instead, record the information and then call Number One and trans-

mit the information to them. Soon! If you cannot reach adjuster number one, then **you** should go out. Service the client first. *Later,* explore why the other person or office was unavailable. Do not convey annoyance to the client! Often, by the time the client fumbles for a pen, your recording will be listing the second person's name and phone number.

In one claim office, Adjuster Smith complained that she always followed Cierpinski and Alberghetti on the recording. She wondered why she was getting all the calls when she was only third on the list. After a while, it dawned on her that clients gave up trying to write down the tongue-twister names and finally decided, "Oh hell, let's just call Smith!"

Tip #35: Be Meticulous in Taking New Loss Information

Be exhaustive in detail when taking down information over the phone during an initial assignment. This will save much time later. Include policy numbers, phone numbers, identifying information regarding vehicles and pinpoint the accident locus. Nothing is more frustrating than circling around and around trying to find an accident scene because the first person transposed numbers! Don't overlook the obvious. Remember to get the name and reporting address of your client. After the dust has settled from the accident investigation, the claim file will have to be reported, and that is when a lot of this information comes in handy.

Tip #36: When in Doubt, Go Out

DO NOT ASK THE CLIENT, "SHOULD I GO OUT?" That is a judgment they are paying YOU to make. Unless the client specifically states in an unsolicited way that you need *not* go out, rest assured the client felt he had good reason to call you. "Everyone has left the scene" is not a good reason for putting a call-in on the back burner until that rainstorm (or your desk) clears. What you can't accomplish at the accident scene you should complete before the start of the next work day.

Tip #37: Consider the Unique Needs of "Call-Out" Clients

Remember that "on-call" clients tend to be high-profile, high-target risks. They carry high liability insurance limits and are likely to be sued. Included here are bus lines and trucking companies. These clients tend to be very hard-nosed and aggressive in their supervision of claims. One brokerage claims supervisor specializing in long-haul trucking losses told me, "I'm tired of being %$#-damned to death every day!" These companies are very demanding and are obsessive about prompt and thorough accident investigations. If you haven't done your homework, or if they smell timidity, they'll sniff out your shortcuts faster than you can say "eighteen-wheeler." Here we are talking about on-the-scene investigations and face-to-face contact. If you don't meet their rigorous standards, you'll quickly find the business going to competitors.

If your office handles truck and cargo losses, advance planning will save you much time when assignments arrive. Gather in advance names, addresses and phone numbers of the following types of companies:

- heavy duty wrecker services
- air-bag/cushion recovery systems
- salvage dealers
- temporary labor pools for loading and unloading trucks
- commercial photographers
- engineers

Learn in advance their after-hour phone numbers. Keep this information in a file folder and keep it with you. Prepare a "call-out" claim kit.

Tip #38: Write Legibly
Beyond the initial assignment, take good, legible notes. There is a chance that the case will be assigned to another adjuster at the start of the next business day. Save him or her lots of wasted effort by recording on claim progress sheets exactly what you have done on the claim. Write legibly or print so that a translator won't be needed to understand the meaning. Nothing is as frustrating a time-waster as not being able to read someone else's writing. Contribute to someone *else's* time management: write legibly or print!

Tip #39: Call in the Reserves!
Know when to call for help. Some cases may transcend your

expertise level or may simply be too large for one adjuster to adequately handle. Examples might include a pollution spill, multiple fatalities or a huge fire loss. It's not a sign of weakness to call for help.

> Justin Adjuster: "Know enough to know when you don't know enough."

Get help from a supervisor or a more experienced adjuster. Better to do this than to try to bluff your way through and later be flirting with an errors-and-omissions claim!

Tip #40: Use Other Claim Offices

Recognize situations warranting referral to another claims office in a different locale. Don't be timid or feel awkward that you might be ruining someone else's day. Situations frequently calling for such referrals include: claimants in transit, buses en route to another geographic area, assignments which unbeknownst to the client fall outside your territory. One major bus company withdrew its entire claims referral business from a state and brought all case-handling in-house. The reason: its outside adjusting company was so concerned about dumping the "inconvenient" assignment on other offices that losses were not promptly investigated.

Time management is a skill applicable to field- as well as in-office work. Like any other skill, it can be learned and reinforced to the point where it becomes second-nature. Analyze how you spend your time outside the office. Do you spend time thinking about the way you schedule appointments? Do you cluster outside appointments together? Do you plan your outside work for times that you know will be light mail days? Examine your calendar or diary for the last three months. What does it show?

Benefits from managing outside time include improved professional productivity. Too often, commuting and waiting time is used only for daydreaming. A little planning for road trips may be your first step toward being a top adjuster. Maybe it will lead to a raise or promotion! The benefits can improve your personal productivity away from the job. With a time management approach, you

should find your road work is less wheel-spinning and more results-oriented.

Besides the obvious productivity advantages from this approach
is the positive feeling of being more in control of your claim files
and your job. Those who fail to think about their use of outside
time are often the same adjusters most frustrated by interruptions.
They are often "behind the eight-ball" and put themselves into
time pressure due to their own procrastination. Granted, some
interruptions are unavoidable. This is inherent in the claims business. Intelligent management of outside time, however, can minimize the prevalence of "rush jobs."

With this should come the peace of mind resulting from having
control over cases, as opposed to them having control over you. A
quiet confidence results from wiser time management. A great part
of the adjuster's job remains to be done outside the office. The
modern adjuster can ill-afford not to wisely manage this time.

NOTES

1. "Coping With the Unfriendly Skies: Airlines' Poor Service Forces
Business Fliers to Alter Travel Habits," *Washington Post*, August 12, 1987,
p. F1.

2. Ibidem

3. "Trapped Behind the Wheel: Clever Commuters Learn to Live in the
Slow Lane," *Time*, July 20, 1987, p. 64.

Chapter Six

Turbo-Charging Your Time Management Skills

Let's now examine some other ways that adjusters can boost their productivity, starting with one area common to all adjuster's jobs ...

Dealing With Lawyers

Virtually all claim professionals deal with lawyers. Sometimes, though, lawyers seem to frustrate the time management efforts of claim professionals. Here are some techniques on dealing with lawyers in ways to maximize your effectiveness.

Tip #1: Go Under Their Heads

Adjusters often feel they waste tremendous amounts of time waiting on attorneys. Adjusters need information to move claims along. How did the accident happen? What are the injuries? What medical reports are available? Who are the treating physicians? Often, busy attorneys will have a secretary, paralegal or clerk assigned to them. In large firms, sometimes a lawyer will have one of *each*. The support staff is often more accessible than the lawyer, more approachable and can often give you much information. Rather than spinning wheels trying to get through to the Important Busy Attorney who never returns calls or answers your mail, don't go over the lawyer's head. Go under it!

What do you need? Index Bureau information on the claimant? A description of the accident? Names of witnesses? The total amount of specials to date? Names of treating physicians? Try to get this from the attorney's secretary or paralegal. Get to know them on a first-name basis. Obviously there are no guarantees, but you may have better success than wasting time chasing a busy attorney. While you won't be negotiating settlement with these individuals, cultivating friendly relations may provide you with an efficient avenue for obtaining needed claim information.

This same approach works for defense counsel as well. Moreover, if you start to feel like you're getting the runaround from them, ask yourself the obvious question, "Why am I using him if he's causing me this kind of headache?" In such a case, firing uncooperative defense lawyers and replacing them with some who will work with you may be a smart time management step.

Some adjusters use attorney intransigence as a "crutch," an excuse for passivity. Instead of aggressively following up, they report, "Attorney Miller is not cooperating ..." or "Attorney Jones will not respond to ... " or, "We have not been able to obtain [information/medicals/specials/a release] from claimant's counsel." Resourceful adjusters find a way around this using creative techniques. That is not to say there aren't lazy attorneys from whom you can get very little. The excuse of lawyer intransigence is overused, however. Counsel may indeed be stubborn, but her staff may be more cooperative. They may even know more about the case than does the attorney. What you cannot obtain through the "front door" you may be able to get through the "back door."

Tip #2: Present a "Negative Option"

Book and record clubs thrive on the "negative option" technique: if you don't reply they take that as an order and they send you a bill with merchandise. The onus is on the receiver to take some affirmative action. Failure to act or respond is interpreted as assent. By doing nothing, the lawyer indicates agreement with your proposal. This may get the attorney's attention and response. For example, if a claim has been dormant for months and you're simply waiting to hear back from claimant's counsel, you can try to smoke him or her out by writing:

> *"I have not heard from you in 6 months. Unless I hear from you within 30 days, I will assume that your client is no longer intent on pursuing this claim ..."*

While lawyers have no legal obligation to reply, as a business practice they may not wish to take any chances. Such a letter may trigger a response, even if the response is, "You are wrong. I still do represent Mr. "X" and will be presenting a settlement demand ..." This may also help if you need to fend off a bad faith claim, showing "reverse bad faith" on the part of the claimant's lawyer.

Tip #3: Document The Non-Response

This may keep you from wasting a lot of time waiting for a reply from a claimant's lawyer. If repeated phone calls and letters are ignored, document these in your file and follow up with the attorney documenting these instances:

> *"This will follow up on my earlier letters of [x,y,z].... to which I have received no reply. Further, my phone calls to you of ... have never been returned. If you still represent Mr. Jones, then please call or write to me within 10 days."*

This approach has some psychological advantage as well. Aside from drawing a response, this kind of letter may also put claimant's counsel on the defensive in later negotiations: another bonanza aside from the time-management benefit. Some adjusters copy the claimant in on this type of letter, but I do not recommend that. While you do want to get a reply to your requests, you do not want to totally alienate the lawyer and destroy any chance of a working relationship on this or future cases. There may also be ethical canons in your jurisdiction barring this type of direct "communications" with a represented claimant.

Tip #4: Try an End-Run — Go Over Their Heads

Use this sparingly or as a last resort. If repeated attempts to elicit a response from a lawyer are consuming much time, try communicating with a partner, a senior partner or a name partner in the firm. Scan the attorney's letterhead up and down. Is there anyone there that you do know well and with whom you have a good working relationship? Casually mention your exasperation in not being able to ever get any answer from Attorney X. Explain why you need to speak with someone there about a claim. Be ready to itemize all the attempts you have made to reach your intended target.

If a partner or associate brings the matter up, this may shame the offending counsel into giving you a reply.

Caveat: carefully weigh how the lawyer might react: considering the attorney's personality, demeanor and the chances you'll have to work with that attorney again. Don't burn bridges if you can avoid it. Someday, you may need a favor from the lawyer. If the issue is important, the counsel is easy-going or you don't think you'll need to deal with that attorney again, then give it a try. In the long run, it will save you time.

Tip #5: Make it Easy for Them

Use the time-honored tactic of fait accompli. Having a hard time getting copies of medical reports and bills out of an attorney? Send out a Medical Authorization form already filled out and ask to have the client sign.

Having trouble getting confirmation of wage loss? Send the lawyer a completed Wage Authorization form.

Have you reached an impasse in settlement discussions? Mail claimant's counsel a check and Release form reflecting your recommended amount, or send a check with a release-type endorsement on the back of the check.

The lawyer can take the easy path of least resistance by accepting the money or can go to the trouble of returning the check and release. In some cases, the sight and feel of a check may persuade the attorney or the claimant to settle. At worst the lawyer rejects this and return it to you, in which case you're no worse off than you were before. In any event, you'll likely get a response.

Use this tactic selectively — in exceptional situations. A lazy claims-person might use this as a substitute for negotiation, which it could become. Use this only where you feel a claim has some settlement value but you cannot get any response after repeated attempts with counsel. Also, do **not** use the tactic with unrepresented claimants! They may cash the check but refuse to sign the release. Then you have problems determining whether or not a legal and binding settlement agreement exists.

Tip #6: Negotiate Efficiently

When negotiating with lawyers, see if you have many cases with the same attorney or law firm. If so, schedule an appointment for a negotiating session with the lawyer. Give that meeting the express purpose of trying to dispose of a number of cases. Certain law firms or lawyers in your area may represent an inordinate amount of claimants. When I supervised workers' compensation for the Washington, D.C. Transit Authority, virtually all claimants were represented by one of two plaintiff firms. Scheduling negotiating sessions with them enabled us to resolve dozens of cases at one sitting. Make each appointment or meeting serve more than one purpose.

Another payoff: momentum you generate in settling the "easier" cases first may carry over to the tougher claims. It also conveys to claimant's counsel your sincere interest in trying to reach an accommodation on each claim. Claimant lawyers often treat you differently once they've met you in person and have spent some time with you negotiating. This may earn you more consideration later in terms of returning phone calls, answering letters and an overall atmosphere of cooperation in future claims.

Do your homework and be prepared to negotiate. If you aren't prepared, don't start. Preparation saves time. If an attorney calls you to discuss settlement on a case you don't feel comfortable with at that time, beg off and tell the lawyer you'll call him back later. Review the file. List the special damages, your arguing points on liability and any special factors. Then, phone the lawyer and say that you've had a chance to review the claim. Have a strategy in mind when you call counsel. If you have an outline in front of you, you will be much more effective and efficient when negotiating settlements. Whether you or the lawyer initiates the topic of settlement, be prepared.

Negotiating claims is a book-length topic in itself, and this does not pretend to be a chronicle of techniques. A few common sense considerations can make you a more efficient negotiator, however.

Tip #7: Pre-empt Stalling Tactics

Beware of lawyers' verbal statements which seem to promise a lot but which are riddled with loopholes:

"I'll take it to my client." Reply: Set a deadline for a response.

"I'll recommend it to my client." Respond: "Well, is there any reason your own client wouldn't follow your advice?"

"I'm waiting for the Release back from my client." Answer: "You represented that the case was settled. We don't want to have to file a Motion to Compel with the court to get the settlement finalized. Please see what you can do."

Certain "throwaway" lines appear to be concessions when in fact they grant little or nothing. Seal off all escape routes that claimant attorneys may try to give themselves that would delay case resolution.

When negotiating, the best time management technique may be to FORGET ABOUT TIME MANAGEMENT!!

Generally, the person under time pressure comes off poorly in negotiations. You're better off if you can put the claimant or claimant's counsel under time pressure and if you act like you've got all the time in the world. Some things shouldn't be hurried, and negotiation is one of them.

Tip #8: Develop a Personal Working Relationship

If you're having a hard time getting phone calls returned or letters answered, maybe it's because you're just another face in the crowd to the claimant's lawyer. Maybe you're not even a face, but just a name. Maybe they don't even recognize your name. Solution: meet personally with the active claimant attorneys. When they have a face to associate with a name, they're much more likely to respond to you. Conversely, it is much more difficult for them to snub you.

The solution: leave the office and meet the key players in the local plaintiff's bar. You shouldn't have any trouble coming up with a reason to visit them, but concoct one if you must. Your personal presence will give you more clout. Your calls may get returned plus you may have an easier time settling cases. All the way around, this saves you time in the long run.

Tip #9: Standardize Defense Attorney Forms

Do you find yourself making the same types of referrals over and over again to defense attorneys? Do you find yourself needing the same type of information from them periodically? If so, take time to standardize referral letters so that you simply plug in the law firm's name and address, name of claimant, insured, date of loss, etc. You can accomplish this on a word-processor.

Also, devise a check-off request form for defense attorneys when you need items such as settlement value, jury verdict range, legal opinion, case status, etc. Leave some blank space for adding specific comments or questions unique to that claim. (See sample below.)

Use this same approach when dealing with claimant lawyers. For example, chances are your response to attorney "representa-

---

SAMPLE RESPONSE TO CLAIMANT ATTORNEY LETTER
OF REPRESENTATION

[date]

Re: Claim Number: _____
              Policy Number: _____
              Insured: _____
              Your Client: _____
              D/Loss: _____
              My File: _____

Dear [lawyer's name]:

We represent the liability insurer for [name of insured] and have just received your recent letter of representation regarding the case of [claimant's name].

Although the events giving rise to this claim occurred about [# of months or years] ago, your letter is my client's first notice of loss. We are currently in the process of investigating this matter.

To that end, you can expedite or delay this process. We would greatly appreciate you forwarding any documentation regarding your client's damages: medical bills, reports, evidence of actual wage loss, medical documentation of disability supporting such wage loss, etc.

As you know, we can likely obtain such information through discovery, but would prefer the faster and less expensive route via informal cooperation.

Should you wish to discuss this matter, then please call me. Thank you for your help and anticipated cooperation.

Sincerely,

[Adjuster's name]

bcc: client

tion" letters say essentially the same things, with some case-to-case variation. Pick examples of your best answers and prepare a form. With a few word changes as to the names and dates, you can quickly standardize letters you send claimant attorneys. [See sample following this page.] Don't advertise that it's a form-type letter, though, even if you suspect the lawyer's letter of representation came off a word-processor. With defense counsel, you have the clout of not paying his bill or not using his services. These levers are not available in dealing with claimant lawyers.

(On a following page is one sample type of "check-off" attorney form.)

Claim professionals not only work with attorneys, but they also deal with a wide range of people in the medical community. Hence our next area of consideration for time management tips ...

Dealing With Doctors & Health Care Providers

Tip #10: Call the Doctor's Secretary

Doctors are as busy, as lawyers, if not busier. They hate paperwork and normally hire a secretary to take care of it. If you need information or clarification from a physician and can't get a reply, follow up by phone with the doctor's secretary. Physicians usually have a medical records clerk who can help. Get to know these people on a first-name basis. If he or she cannot readily find the answer, they can relay your query to the doctor and get back to you. This saves the physician time and saves you time that would otherwise be spent in futile written follow-up.

If your office or company uses the doctor for independent medical exams, don't hesitate to subtly bring that up. Don't be heavy-handed about this, though. Make clear you are not trying to pressure for a favorable opinion necessarily — just a reply to your question or request.

Tip #11: Know When to Call the Doctor

Generally, you'll get nowhere if you try calling a doctor between 9:30 a.m. and 4:30 p.m. You have a better chance of getting through if you phone before 9:30 a.m. or after 4:30 p.m. Alternatively, ask the staff when the best time is to call the doctor. Physicians are more accessible at certain times than others. Think before calling!

Adjusters are frequently timid about talking with physicians or "pushing too hard" to get reasonable inquiries answered. Claimspeople are often still intimidated by physicians, many of whom still harbor a "God complex" and consider insurance claims people some lower form of life on the biological scale. Somehow, adjusters overcome their initial fright of dealing with attorneys until it becomes second nature. Talking to doctors is another hurdle which good adjusters must overcome. You're a professional too, and there's no reason to let the letters M.D. intimidate you.

Tip #12: Make a "Telephone Appointment"

Find out from the doctor's secretary what time the physician will be available to speak. Ask the secretary to have the doctor expect a call from you at that time, and follow up. Prepare your questions in advance, since physicians are very time-conscious, suffer fools poorly and generally are impatient with adjusters who don't know what they're doing. Project an air of competence and confidence. Refuse to be cowed.

Tip #13: Schedule an Appointment to Meet

As in the case of an attorney, sometimes the prospect of a face-to-face meeting will prompt a physician to relent and return your phone call. In some cases, though, there will be little alternative to making an appointment to meet with the doctor. Be prepared though: you'll probably have to pay doctors for their time.

Tip #14: Set Up an IME

Rather than waste time trying to pry information out of a recalcitrant doctor, send the claimant for an independent medical exam with a specialist of your choice. Make sure it's a physician with whom you have a good working relationship, so there won't be any problem in receiving a prompt report that addresses the questions you ask. You are not seeking a "yes-man" or at least that should not be your aim. What you want are key questions answered in a straightforward manner. IME arrangements can often be streamlined and standardized. (What follows is a sample of one IME letter.)

SAMPLE INQUIRY LETTER
TO DEFENSE ATTORNEY

TO: [Name of defense attorney/law firm]

RE: Claim Number: _____
    Insured: _____
    Claimant/Plaintiff: _____
    D/Loss: _____
    Your File: _____

LITIGATED CASE INQUIRY

_____ Please provide a current status report on this case.

_____ Please provide me with copies of prior reports on this claim.

_____ Please copy me in on future reports and correspondence.

_____ Complete the attached Case Evaluation and return it to
        me within 30 days.

_____ Please reference the above claim number on all reports,
        bills and correspondence.

_____ Please review and adhere to the attached Litigation
        Guidelines.

_____ Advise re: total legal fees & expenses on case to date.

_____ Please submit a written discovery plan.

_____ Please complete and return the attached Litigation Plan & Budget.

_____   Other:_____

_____

REMARKS:

BY: _____

Attachment(s)

CC:

SAMPLE "IME LETTER" FOR WORKERS' COMPENSATION CLAIMS

[Date]

Re: Claim Number: _____
                     Policy Number: _____
                     Employer: _____
                     Employee:_____
                     D/Loss: _____
                     Our File: _____

Dear Dr. _____:

We handle workers' compensation cases for [employer's name], one of whose employees, [claimant's name], seeks workers' compensation benefits arising from an alleged on-the-job incident on [date of loss].

We seek an independent, objective and up-to-date assessment of this employee's condition. To this end, we have taken the liberty of scheduling for the employee an independent medical examination for [date and time] at [doctor's address].

By copy of this letter, we are notifying [claimant's name] of the appointment and ask that he/she call your office and mine in advance if the appointment cannot be kept or requires rescheduling.

We would appreciate a narrative report covering: diagnosis, prognosis, objective findings compared to subjective complaints, assessment of disability of any, return to work estimate, causal connection to employment, degree of permanency if any, recommended course of treatment and any other observations which you feel are pertinent.

Attached are medical records regarding the medical care and treatment rendered to date. Please call me if you have any questions. Thank you for your help.

Sincerely,

[Adjuster's name]

Enclosures: Background material

cc: claimant and/or claimant's attorney
     State compensation Board or Commission

bcc: client

Chapter Seven

The Benevolent Dictator

Let's look at some practical dictation tips ...

Tip #1: Dictate Instead of Writing

Mouths move faster than hands. You can talk faster than you can write. Early in your career, develop the habit of dictating reports, letters, memoranda. It will initially feel awkward. Everyone feels this way. If you wear glasses, you might recall that when you first got them, you felt very self-conscious, as if everyone was looking at you. Pretty soon, though, the glasses got to be second-nature and you no longer felt like a geek. The same is true with dictating. After a little time, you'll be much more efficient in answering and generating needed correspondence through dictation. Talking into a machine is preferable to tieing up a secretary's time. By using a hand-held dictaphone, you don't need two people at the same time.

Efficient Dictation

A few preliminary steps will help you sail through dictation. Here are some pointers:

Tip #2: Gather Your Materials Before Dictating

Make sure you have all the needed materials in front of you. Nothing is as frustrating or time-wasting as having to get up in mid-sentence to check on an address, the content of a relevant statute or the address of a key witness.

Tip #3: Plan Your Comments

Know beforehand what you are going to say. This sounds obvious but it is amazing how many adjusters just press the "on" button and start rambling. An ounce of preparation pays off. Outline in advance the points you want to cover and *then* — and only then — dictate.

Tip #4: S-p-e-l-l Tough Words and Names
Spell out proper names and legal and medical terms. This saves time having to send back or correct typed documents. It will also earn you goodwill from the transcriptionists!

Tip #5: Cluster Dictation Jobs for One Time
Cluster your dictation tasks for one part of the day, if possible, and go through it all at that time.

Tip #6: Use the "Salami Technique" on Dictation
If you have a lengthy report that you've been delaying, break it down into separate segments. Dictate three captions, take a break, and then come back to it. Do this until you finish the report. (P.S.: Use a separate cassette tape so you don't back up other, shorter pieces of dictation.)

Tip #7: Be Concise
Make the report concise. If there is no way to condense, consider a one-page cover letter with your conclusions and recommendations. Make the "bottom line" the top line, giving your findings, conclusions or recommendations in summary or "bullet" form. As an attachment to that top sheet, make the lengthy report an appendix. This will be available to the recipient if she wants to slog through it or explore the reasoning behind your findings and recommendations. Clients and higher-ups don't have time to read your version of "War and Peace." Since they are very busy, don't make them wade through eight single-spaced pages to reach your main idea.

Tip #8: Offer Solutions — Not Tea and Sympathy
Don't spend eight pages telling the client it has a problem. Tell them how you're going to solve it, or what you recommend. Give advice, not sympathy. Stick your neck out.

"Behold the lowly turtle — he only makes progress when he sticks his neck out."

Tip #9: Write Right

Write right, and you will save yourself, your company and your clients time.

Warning: people tend to be more verbose when dictating than when writing. Avoid diarrhea of the mouth. Keep it concise. Strive for economy. Keep correspondence to one page in length. Looking at some claim files, one would think adjusters were getting paid by the pound!

Tip #10: Avoid Dictation Perfectionism

You're doing a report, not vying for the Nobel Literature Prize. Avoid perfectionism. Perfectionism paralyzes some claims people to the point where they put off dictation. Relax! Think of this as your draft. You can always proofread. With today's memory typewriters and word-processors, making corrections and revisions is a snap. (Don't overdo the revision process, either, though. Check for spelling, grammar, punctuation and brevity, but don't waste time agonizing over a draft.)

Tip #11: Use "Adjuster Shorthand"

Save time when making file notes or taking notes over the phone by using what I call "adjuster shorthand." Some examples:

P/L	Proof of Loss
FTY	Failure to Yield
L	left
R	right
U	up
D	down
A/R	accident report
AP	appraise
S/S	signed statement
R/S	recorded statement
appt	appointment
attny	attorney
acv	actual cash value
ttd	temporary total disability
ppd	permanent partial disability
ptd	permanent total disability

tpd	temporary partial disability
dr	doctor
<	less than
>	greater than
OLT	owners, landlords & tenants
Ø	nothing
↑	increase
↓	decrease
CGL	comprehensive general liability
clmt	claimant
insd	insured
IME	independent medical exam
WC	workers' compensation
subro	subrogation
MP	medical payments
l-s	lumbosacral
BC/BS	Blue Cross/Blue Shield
A&H	accident and health
GI	gastrointestinal
IC	independent contractor
S/R	status report
F/U	follow up
w/	with
Δ	change
=	is
≠	is not
w/o	without
RTW	return to work
ded	deductible
U/M	uninsured motorist
?	question
⟶	cause
⟶/	did not cause

These are just some possibilities and this list is by no means exhaustive. By using abbreviations and adjuster shorthand, you reduce the time spent writing in the file about what was done.

This leaves you more time to *do* instead of write. Make sure that whatever abbreviations you use are legible and understandable, both to you and your supervisor!

Tip #12: Diagram Efficiently

Is diagramming a lost art? Adjusters often dread drawing diagrams of accident scenes because they "take too long." Admittedly, diagramming is not the sexiest part of the adjuster's job, but it has to be done, especially for vehicular and premises-liability claims. There are a few simple steps, however, which can make the process more efficient.

Tip #13: Get Time-Saving Diagramming Tools

Make sure you have the right tools. You'll probably need at minimum some templates depicting automobiles, landmarks, drawing curves, etc. Any drafting supply store should have a good variety of templates which will make the job easier, if not downright fun. You'll need a ruler and perhaps a protractor as well. A few companies sell stick-ons for diagrams. These come in a kit and include hundreds of reusable adhesives useful in illustrating how an accident occurred. Invest in a rolling type of measuring wheel, which is much more exact than trying to pace off measurements. Some police supply stores and mail order houses sell these. (Among the latter: Razak Engineering Company, Inc., 1305 E. Waterman, Wichita, KS, 67211, (316) 265-4911.)

Tip #14: Do A Rough Draft of the Diagram — Polish Later

At the accident scene, make a rough sketch of the locus and take key measurements. When you return to the office, prepare a finished or more polished diagram while the layout is still fresh in your mind. If you wait a week, you may forget about the placement of Stop Signs, Speed Limit signs, etc.

Efficient Statement-Taking

Since so much of the adjuster's time is taken up with statements, it makes sense to think about how they can be obtained efficiently. Some suggestions:

Tip #15: Do Your Statement Homework

Review in advance the key questions you want to ask. What are the important points you must cover? Surprisingly, many adjusters never study a statement outline once they finish training class. No matter what experience level, adjusters should review in advance the questions they wish to ask. This helps get to the point and avoid wasting the deponent's time, and yours.

Tip #16: Do Prep Work on the Signed Statement Sheets

Number the signed statement sheets in advance and clearly label the area on the bottom line where the person should sign.

Tip #17: Have Plenty of Statement Tools

Bring along some extra pens. You invite wasted time and embarrassment by asking a claimant in the middle of a statement to borrow a pen because yours ran out of ink and you didn't think to bring a spare. You've not only run out of ink, but out of credibility as well!

Tip #18: Give Your Hardware a Pre-Flight Check

When taking recorded statements, make sure before and after that your recorder and cassette are in good working order. This saves you having to go back and do the whole statement over again. You may not be able to get someone to give you the same statement twice! Have extra cassettes on hand. Cassettes often are limited to 30 minutes and not all statements will finish neatly within this time frame. Make sure you have extra batteries for your recorder and an AC adapter cord as well. To avoid wasting time hunting down extra cassettes in the middle of a statement, keep or carry with you plenty of unused spares.

Tip #19: Summarize as You Go

Make notes as you go along during a recorded statement. Some adjusters loathe writing up recorded statement summaries. They love the efficiency of recorded statements but hate the "scut work" of summarizing them later. One solution: write it as you go along. One pitfall is that the adjuster's concentration is not on the questions and content but more on keeping up with the deponent's answers.

Tip #20: Dictate a Summary While It's Fresh in Your Mind

Another tactic is to dictate the summary of the R/S right afterward, while it's fresh in your mind. This is faster than laboriously hand-writing a summary and is often more legible as well.

Tip #21: Kill Two Birds With One Stone

When meeting with people to obtain statements, seize the moment to get further needed material and information: a signed Medical and Wage Authorization; copies of medical bills or reports; repair bills; photographs of damage; leads for names of other witnesses; gauge settlement expectations; etc. Make your meeting serve a number of purposes in addition to getting a statement. Kill two or more birds with the same stone.

Dealing with Interruptions

Are you plagued by interruptions? Is your time frittered away by drop-in visitors and impromptu meetings? Here are some tips on keeping these from consuming too much of your time.

Tip #22: Diagnose Your Sources of Interruptions

Are they from ...

- Your staff? Maybe you haven't adequately briefed them on what is expected. Maybe you spoon-feed them answers to questions they should find on their own. Encourage your staff to save up a number of topics to discuss with you at one time. Examine your own management style. It might unwittingly invite interruptions. Encourage self-reliance on your staff's part.
- Your clients? Maybe you're not communicating with them, making it inevitable that they will follow up to find out what is going on with their losses. Perhaps a better diary system and regular reporting could squelch these interruptions.

If these "interruptions" are new case assignments, there's not a lot you can do. If you're an independent adjuster, thank your lucky stars for these types of "interruptions"!

- Your boss? If you hear, "Where is the [x]" or "I expected to hear from you," then the problem isn't the telephone or interruptions, but *your* lack of follow-up and inability to complete projects on time. Anticipate!

111

Some bosses seem to secretly enjoy crises, believing that they work best under optimum pressure. Unfortunately, these managers also assume that everyone around them also works better under pressure.

> On December 1, manager "Chipper" Uris officially learned that his claim office won the claim service contract for the local municipality. His branch would take over close to 6,000 runoff cases and pick up new ones as well. The first planning meeting with the supervisory staff was held almost 3 weeks later, the day before the trucks arrived to deliver the files. The office was topsy turvy. Adjusters worked almost around the clock during the holidays setting up cases. Tempers flared. Many quit. Lack of planning hampered the takeover. Chipper thrived on crises, though, and waited till the last minute to plan this massive case takeover.

Interruptions and crises are not merely problems. They are *symptoms* that something is awry in managing your time. Management sage Peter Drucker states, "The recurrent crisis is simply a symptom of slovenliness and laziness."

Despite this, some bosses and adjusters thrive on crises. They are galvanized by the supercharged atmosphere and work best (or feel they do) when "the heat is on" and events reach this critical stage. Analyze the underlying causes of crises. Adopt procedures for dealing with recurrent crises. Emergency rooms deal with crises every hour but have prepared protocols on dealing with life and death matters. Ask yourself: What are the Claim Department's recurrent crises? On the scene investigations? Claim audits? Takeovers of large new accounts? Systematize a way to deal with each. Attack the causes of crises and you'll spend less time fighting fires!

Tip #23: Structure Your Workspace to Discourage Interruptions

Organize your desk or work space so as to invite privacy. Some desks and work spaces almost invite drop-in visitors. Does your desk face the door? Is it located near your office entrance? This may encourage people to make eye contact and drop in. Consider having your desk face away from the door or at an angle to it.

Tip #24: Close the Door ... Occasionally

Don't overlook the obvious: close your door once and a while for limited periods of time. Situate a secretary's desk near the entrance to your door so unscheduled or unwanted visitors can be intercepted. Enlist the help of a gate-keeper, but not so much that people feel deterred from bringing you bad news and problems.

Tip #25: Get Comfortable, But Not TOO Comfortable

Does your desk or office layout invite distractions by placement of mementos or knickknacks? Put them on a side table or in a less conspicuous place. Personalize your office space and feel at home ... but not *too much* at home. You need not have a spartan office to efficiently organize your work area.

Tip #26: Beware of Bull Sessions

Avoid "war stories" and adjuster bull sessions: "Hey Joe, lemme' tell you about this case I just got ..." "That reminds me of this one time this claimant ..." And so on and so on, becoming a contest of "Can you top this?" Claims people love to swap war stories of unusual claims, situations, My Most Difficult Claimant, etc. Nothing is inherently wrong with this. These sessions are entertaining and often therapeutic, but can easily grow out of control and waste time.

Tip #27:Hold Stand-Up Meetings

Hold stand-up meetings. These take less time than sit-down confabs. If you feel a conversation has run on long enough, rise from your chair. Nonverbal cues like this will usually prompt the other person to wind up their business. Rid your office or desk area of excess chairs. People will be much less likely to drop in and sit down to "shoot the breeze."

Tip #28: Just Say "No" to Drop-In Solicitors

Sometimes, vendors purveying services will drop in on you because they "just happened to be in the neighborhood." Such vendors may include rental car companies, contractors, detective agencies, rehabilitation companies and the like. They wouldn't think of just "dropping in" on a doctor or lawyer, but think nothing about doing this to a busy claim professional. Do not reward or encourage this practice! Thank them for stopping by but tell them you're sorry you weren't expecting them and are pretty busy. Suggest if they want to set up a time to meet, then you would be open to that. If they have any sensitivity, they'll get your message. (Postscript: If they're so dense that they don't get your drift, why would you want to buy their services anyway?)

Tip #29: Engage Your Secretary — Any Secretary — as an Accomplice

If visitors — scheduled or unscheduled — overstay their welcome and you must get back to work, arrange in advance for a secretary to give you a signal. For instance, instruct your secretary in advance to buzz you when 30 minutes or an hour is up, telling you that your next appointment is coming up. The appointment may be with *yourself* to get some work done, but this will normally cue visitors to wind up their business and leave. This pre-arranged technique is especially useful if you know in advance that the visitor is long-winded.

Tip #30: Beg Off and Defer the Discussion

If you're in mid-task and just cannot tolerate an interruption, ask the person if you can get back to them. Make yourself a note and be sure you do get back to them when promised! When you do get back with them, do so on *their* turf. When business is finished, it is easier for you to leave their work space than for you to try to get them to leave yours. Alternately, make an appointment with the person at a time more convenient for you.

Tread carefully here, though. Claims people are in a service business. Some drop-in interruptions are an inevitable part of the job. One must be accessible to clients, supervisors, co-workers, etc. Managers and supervisors must be accessible to their staff and cannot give the impression that they are "in the way." Be sensitive to appearances so you maintain the good will of colleagues, your staff and clients.

Tip #31: Leave Breathing Room in Your Schedule

Leave some "breathing room" in your schedule and avoid the temptation to become over-booked.

For the sake of time management, do not become anti-social.

Economist Jeremy Rifkin laments that "despite our alleged efficiency, we seem to have less time for ourselves and far less time for each other." In a sense, getting along with **people** is the ultimate form of time management for claims professionals. Without that ability, no amount of time management skill will help.

Stopping Procrastination

I've been putting this topic off for long enough. You know you're getting old when you decide to procrastinate but then never get around to it. You needn't be old, though. Even young claims professionals manage to procrastinate. The tendency to defer gratification and to procrastinate are closely related. As psychiatrist M. Scott Peck observes, "Some people always eat the icing before the cake."

What do you eat first, the icing or the cake? Adjusters often take the path of least resistance by focusing on "icing matters," postponing the more difficult tasks at hand. Resist the temptation to always start with the easy tasks.

Resist the temptation to always pick the low-hanging fruit.

The reach must extend upward, to the tougher tasks. Adjusters sitting down at their desk at the start of the day may pick up some simple tasks — routine paperwork, for instance — at first to "ease into the day." There is nothing inherently wrong with this, until it starts absorbing most of the morning. Claim professionals must guard against this habit developing to the point where they lose sight of the genuinely important and urgent matters before them.

> *QUINLEY'S TIME MANAGEMENT AXIOM 47:*
> The urgent is not always important and the
> important is rarely urgent.

Since claim professionals deal with upset people, there is a great temptation to procrastinate. Investigations must be completed. Forms must be filed. Inevitably, special projects creep up. How to avoid the "Scarlet O'Hara Syndrome" which puts off everything until tomorrow? Here are some answers:

Tip #32: Break it Down!

Shades of the salami technique here. Break the task down into bite-sized bits. Dissect the job and attack it a little at a time. This is sometimes known as the "salami technique." For a complex new claim assignment, this might involve sitting down with the file and listing 1...2...3... each and every component that needs to be done and keeping it posted prominently in the file.

Tip #33: Incentivize Yourself With Rewards

Reward yourself for accomplishing various checkpoints. This reward can take the form of a candy bar, coffee break, a walk around the block, etc. For bigger accomplishments, give yourself bigger rewards. Develop a habit of positive reinforcement.

Tip #34: Visualize

Envision in your mind how nice the completed project will look. Wouldn't that thick file look nice with a "closed" buck slip on it? How about your name at the top of adjuster rankings for closings at month's end? Visualize the completed job!

Tip #35: Set a Deadline

Give yourself a deadline. You probably won't have to do this too much, since various deadlines are inherent in the claims professional's job. If you're not given one though, give yourself one, or make yours a few days ahead. That way you'll be more likely to finish on time.

Tip #36: Buy in Bulk

Managers, supervisors and adjusters spend time stocking an office with needed supplies. Is there any way to reduce this time? Yes! Certain adjusting supplies are periodically replenished: camera film, pens, writing pads, etc. Explore large bulk purchases of these items through mail order office supply houses. If your area has a Price Club, Sam's Warehouse, B.J.'s, Costco, join up. By buying in bulk or by mail you save time shopping for office supplies and you'll probably save money too. Make sure the claim office management is aware of these purchasing options.

Meeting Mastery

Tip #37: Conduct Painless Meetings

Claims people attend many meetings, some of which they can avoid and some which they cannot. Claims people convene meetings to discuss office policies, company policies, client instructions, claim education and specific files. Meetings not only consume time, but also money. Consider a typical meeting among a claims manager and a staff of one assistant manager and three supervisors. Assume the salaries are:

Claims Manager $65,000

Assistant Manager $35,000

Supervisors (3) $30,000 each

At this rate, each minute is "worth" well over a dollar, making the cost of the meeting almost $100 an hour! Think of meeting time as money and it gives more of an incentive to keep them brief and to a minimum.

Is there any way to keep meetings from dragging on and wasting everyone's time? Yes!

Tip #38: Have and Distribute in Advance a Written Agenda

If you're the one holding the meeting, always have a written agenda. This will help prevent the meeting from turning into a "bull session." Have some specific topics you plan to discuss. Distribute copies of the agenda *in advance* of the meeting so all will know what is to be covered and will have a chance to formulate some thoughts.

Tip #39: Keep a Small Guest List

Keep meeting size small.

A corollary to Murphy's Law is "Shanahan's Law," which states that the length of a meeting rises with the square of the number of people present.

An inverse relationship also exists between the size of the meeting and the effectiveness. Invite or require only those people who must attend. If a meeting focuses on new settlement techniques, is it really necessary to have appraisers and clerical staff present? Be selective in the people asked to attend.

Tip #40: Don't Meet Because It's the Thing to Do

Have a genuine need for a meeting. Are you conferring out of habit, or is there a real need? Is it part of the "if-it's-Monday-we-must-be-meeting" syndrome?

> *Claims Manager Billy Bob required all supervisors to meet with their respective staffs each Monday morning. Usually supervisors had no problems generating ideas but occasionally there seemed to be little or nothing to discuss. Billy Bob berated a supervisor who did not turn in the regular Monday morning meeting outline. Soon thereafter, all supervisors decided to meet every Monday, whether or not there was a genuine need. Supervisors and adjusters grew resentful of this periodic time-waster, but Manager Billy Bob saw only that his supervisory staff submitted weekly outlines. All Billy Bob cared about was that meetings were held and their contents outlined on a form he devised.*

The preceding is a classic example of form championing over substance. Give your office management discretion over when or whether to hold a meeting. Don't hold them just to hold them. If there's nothing to discuss or not enough to require a quorum, save everyone some time and wait till you have enough topics to discuss.

Tip #41: Bring Closure

Come to conclusions and recommendations. A meeting should not turn into a group therapy session. What actions will come out of it? Make it specific and concrete. Assign follow-up tasks. Set deadlines for action and for reporting back. Follow through!

Tip #42: Hold Unstructured Meetings

Hold stand-up meetings, quick impromptu meetings or hallway meetings. These all tend to take less time than your usual sit-down gatherings.

Tip #43: Be Punctual — Start and STOP on Time!

Start and stop on time. If the meeting is to start at 8:30 a.m., start it then. Do not say, "We have a few people missing so I'll give them a little more time." Why penalize the people who showed up on time and reward latecomers? Be punctual in starting on time. Make it known that 8:30 a.m. means 8:30 a.m. and no later. Wrap up on time. If there are eight topics to cover during a 30-minute meeting, then you don't have the luxury of spending 15 minutes on the first two. Letting people know that the meeting will last 30 minutes gives everyone an incentive to make their point soon, and briefly.

Another way to make sure meetings end on time, according to one consultant, is to serve plenty of coffee and give no coffee breaks!

Tip #44: Cope Constructively If Meetings Bleed Your Time

If you're the one being called to meetings and have no control over that, what can you do? Grin and bear it. Try to learn something from the meeting. If you know these meeting are regular, write down topics you wish to raise. If all is lost and the meeting has no relevance for you, discretely make notes as to your agenda, things to follow up on, etc. You can look attentive and all the while be thinking about your next appointment or a new claim assignment. Use this time!

Managing Your Boss

Be a time-saver instead of a time-waster to your boss. Obviously, the best way to do this is to do such a good job that there's never any cause for complaint about your work. Beyond that, though, you can avoid annoying habits which drain boss' time.

Tip #45: Don't Over-Impose on Your Boss' Time

Don't waste your boss' time. Keep it brief. Don't ask, "Can you spare a minute?" and then steal sixty. If it's a quick question, make it quick. Most bosses profess an "open door policy." Don't take this literally as an invitation to walk in at any time. Be considerate. Keep lines of communications open with your boss, but cut short the bull sessions. Of course, if your boss LIKES bull sessions — adapt!

Tip #46: Put Out Feelers and Tune Your Antennae

Ask the boss if he or she has time to talk. If the boss seems to be in the middle of a project, pick up on that. Does the boss have stacks of paper on the desk or look preoccupied? Is there a big home-office project looming? You don't have to be telepathic to notice when it's a bad time to interrupt the boss. Ask if you can make an appointment or ask if you should check back at a later time.

Tip #47: Delegate

Supervisors and managers should make sure that they're not engaged in activities which can and should be performed by someone down in the chain of command. Many newly-promoted supervisors cling to vestiges of their former jobs and thereby waste time. New managers may under-delegate. You know you are under-delegating when any of the following trouble signs appear:

- handling many claims yourself;
- reserving the "choice" cases for yourself; or
- getting directly involved in you staff's files and cases when there is no need.

Continually ask yourself: "Do I really need to be doing this? Could this be done just as well by someone on my staff?" You do your staff a disservice too by not utilizing them more.

> *Once she became claims manager, Jennifer set out to improve her office's file quality. Though she had a capable staff of adjusters, she gave the heaviest cases to herself. She encouraged adjusters to come to her with questions, bypassing her two supervisors. She soon was logging more time in the office than anyone else. Her marketing calls fell behind, and the further behind she got, the more she procrastinated. File quality improved, but her incoming case volume dropped. She always thought quality was key, but in light of her office's dwindling profits, she was starting to have second thoughts.*

Re-examine your job to see if any parts can and should be delegated. Caveat: delegation should not become a technique for dumping on subordinates the nasty jobs which you can't stomach. Parcel out the good with the bad and you can multiply your effectiveness.

Chapter Eight

Staying On The Fast Track

Time management is not an end in itself, but rather a means to an end. Intelligently managing time helps adjusters excel in their careers, and to fit those careers within the larger context of a satisfying life. Time *mis*management lets the job absorb more of one's life than is healthy. Time management is a life skill, not merely a job skill. Nor is it a skill applicable solely to one's day-to-day job demands. Many activities not required by the job are essential for career advancement. Like what, you ask?

For starters, continuing education is a requisite for career advancement and professionalism. You are obviously interested in advancing your career, or else you wouldn't be reading this book in the first place. The claims profession, once seen as a seat-of-the-pants vocation, often struggles to overcome an image associated with bill collectors and used car salesmen.

Ongoing education is a fact of modern business life for aiming for the fast track, with the insurance industry being no exception. Time management helps you stay abreast and move ahead. Many claims people lament that, with such demanding jobs, the study needed for continuing education is an unfair intrusion into their personal lives. Personal and professional lives definitely must be balanced, but one can be an insurance professional without totally sacrificing leisure time. Time management is a tool for this, and those who use time management give themselves a competitive advantage in the insurance marketplace.

Those wishing to do more than just get by, those who want to get ahead and be on the fast track, the movers and shakers within the insurance industry — these professionals will keep up through four main ways:

(1) continuing education courses and programs
(2) professional journals and publications
(3) professional associations
(4) seminars and meetings

Family or personal life need not be sacrificed in order to pursue these paths, though. The key is managing time.

How do claim professionals do this while sharpening their professional skills?

Continuing Education

Opportunities for ongoing training for claims professionals take the following forms: in-house training programs, IIA-CPCU programs, formal degree programs. Let's look at some specifics.

Tip #1: Take Advantage of In-House Training Programs

The claims industry offers a wide variety of in-house programs, ranging from correspondence courses to special off-site schools where employees are sent. The Travelers unveiled an extensive educational facility in Hartford in 1986. That same year, Adjuster Insurance School Inc. in San Diego, Calif. established a combination correspondence and residency training course for company and independent adjusters. In his book *Megatrends,* author John Naisbitt argues that businesses will soon assume much of the educational role once shouldered by colleges and universities. Most in-house programs are tailored to the specific needs of the company developing them. This can be a strength and a weakness.

Advantages of in-house programs include:

- a high degree of flexibility and the ability (especially if a correspondence course is involved) to work at one's own pace;
- courses often involve either no examination or an "open book" type of exam (very handy for those who do not test well); and
- programs parallel specific company procedures or lines of coverage which may be unaddressed or barely mentioned in industry-wide programs.

In-house programs suffer from the drawback that they are often unrecognized on an industry-wide basis. This is more important if a job change is eventually contemplated. Completing eight correspondence courses at XYZ Adjusting Company may have little weight when you go to apply for a claim examiner position with, say, the Chubb. Credentials derived from completing an in-house program may not be as universally recognized or valued as those from a more well-known designation.

Nevertheless, advancement within many companies often hinges on finishing certain in-house programs. Complete them! Often, you have no choice if you want to advance. Some time management suggestions for in-house correspondence-type courses:

Tip #2: Go Easy at First

Begin with baby steps before you start to walk. Walk before you run. Jog short distances before you try a marathon. If it's your first course, start with one of the easiest, most fundamental programs. Course synopses are often available in advance from one's Training Department. For an adjuster moving into serious workers' compensation claims for the first time, for instance, it makes little sense to enroll in "Advanced Workers' Compensation" when a course in "Basic Medical Terminology" is available.

Tip #3: Break it Down

"How do you eat a 200-lb. turkey? One bite at a time!" Use the "salami technique" and break your study schedule down into bite-sized bits. Don't try to knock off a chapter each day. Set a modest target of, say, five or ten pages per day. How long can it take to read ten pages?! At ten pages per day, you'll probably be through with the core readings well in advance of the exam date. This allows you more time to review and study for the exam. One consultant estimates that if you devote 15 minutes a day to reading, you will complete the equivalent of 52 books a year! Get going!

Tip #4: Build a Daily Study Habit

Answer one study guide question each day or invest 30 minutes per day. Make it the same time each day, so it becomes a habit. Psychologists say it takes about 30 days to build a new habit. Apply this concept to studying. Pretty soon studying becomes an ingrained habit, and you won't need iron will-power to just do it.

Study at the same time and at the same location each day, if possible. Some adjusters use lunch time for studying. Travelling on a plane or subway allows time for study, normally free of interruptions. Do it daily!

Tip #5: Give Yourself a Target

Deadlines have a way of generating energy. Give yourself a specific target date for completion. Write it down on paper. Post a study schedule at your desk with your completion date.

Stick your neck out. Announce to your family or colleagues that you're going to finish a course or program by a certain date. Making the goal public is another way of helping you stick with the program. Register early for the exam, as soon as you receive the registration packet. This lends an air of finality to your commitment and avoids the temptation of not sitting for the exam. Commit yourself and register early! You also avoid late registration fees, so this is another way that saving time also saves money.

Many claim professionals will begin their continuing education efforts through in-house courses developed by their own employers. Often this whets the appetite to work toward one of the insurance designations recognized industry-wide. This brings us to the next topic ...

Professional Designations

Tip #6: Get Involved with IIA/CPCU Courses

For the past 20 years, the standard of continuing education accomplishment within the industry has been the Chartered Property Casualty Underwriter (CPCU) designation and specialty designations offered by the Insurance Institute of America (IIA). The Associate in Claims designation and the CPCU initials are widely recognized as stepping-stones to advancement within the insurance industry and are well-recognized within the claims and insurance fields. Applying time management principles can improve the odds of completing these programs with the maximum payback.

Tip #7: Use Free or Inexpensive Study Aids

Some aids don't cost a penny. The Institute's own materials represent an often-overlooked resource. These materials include:

• Yearly course catalogs. These are free by writing to the Insurance Institute of America, 720 Providence Road, Malvern, PA, 19355-0770. The catalogs provide, among other things, guidelines about course sequence, so you'll know where to begin if you're interested in starting a program.

• The Malvern Examiner. Also published quarterly and free from the IIA. The Examiner offers practical tips on how to prepare for examinations and how to devise a "study strategy." Articles include, "Taking the Fear Out of Independent Study" and "Top Achievers Tout Tips."

• Preparation Handbook-Study Skills Guide for CPCU/IIA Students. Available for $3.00 from the IIA. More "how to" suggestions on preparing for exams, with a pre-printed form helpful for blocking out study time well in advance.

• Course Guides. Currently priced at $14 each. Don't overlook the obvious! Each course guide chapter presents one of (usually) 12 lessons in summary form, complete with a vocabulary/terminology list and practice study questions.

The Institute also offers a self-evaluation program which you should consider. As a student, you complete a confidential questionnaire and mail it to the Institute. One of the Institute's staff will privately review it and provide you with written advice, including a recommended sequence of courses. All this is confidential, and may offer advice on the best sequence of courses to take, thereby making the most efficient use of your study time.

A mini-industry has risen to fill the needs of those preparing for IIA/CPCU examinations. Often these are high-priced packages including: practice exams, workbooks, cassette tapes, and sample examination questions and answers. The Institute does not endorse or recommend any of these study aids, but that doesn't mean you shouldn't consider them. (A listing of some of these outside aids follows in a few pages.)

Tip #8: Compose a Study Schedule
Armed with the Institute's own materials, apply many time management ideas to successful course completion. These guidelines

are useful regardless if one is self-studying or taking a class.

One key idea is to map out a schedule and timetable. Simply calculate the number of days or weeks remaining until the exam, then divide this by the number of lessons in the course (usually 12 for IIA; 15 for CPCU) or the number of pages of text to read. This tells you how to pace yourself, and how much reading per day or per week you need to stay on target. Recruit other people who are self-studying the same class and form a study group. Quiz each other, discuss the readings, clarify questions and provide a support group to stay motivated through the exam preparation process.

Tip #9: Invest 30 Minutes a Day

Read for 30 minutes per day. Make it the same 30 minutes per day, if possible. Make it a habit. Consider getting up 30 minutes earlier or going to bed 30 minutes later each night.

In an extra hour [a day] you could clear your desk or learn French or take up the piano or pursue some other hobby or skill you've thought long about. One and a half hours a day would give you an additional 547 hours a year, the equivalent of an extra month of working hours. *That's like adding a year to every 12 years you will live.*[1]

> *Do this daily, and you give yourself the equivalent of almost an entire extra workday each week. What will YOU do with this extra seven hours? Is 30 minutes a day really too much to ask for career advancement?*

Tip #10: Use the Institute Course Guides

Fully use the Course Guide, one of the best — if not THE best — study aid available right under your nose. Despite the availability of commercial study aids, this book remains the best preparation road map. For each reading assignment, the Course Guide offers vocabulary terms, practice questions and exam-calibre discussion questions. Give them a workout!

Tip #11: Don't Double-Up

Avoid doubling up on courses. Yes, a few rare individuals successfully pull this off, but — by and large — it does not work. Doubling or tripling up may miss the point of the whole program:

to learn and retain insurance knowledge, not to rush through as quickly as possible. These programs are distance races, not sprints. You're not likely to speed through them, though one occasionally hears about someone who sat for all exams at one time and passed. (Or, was it "passed out"?!)

Even if it succeeds, doubling up is usually an unpleasant grind. If the preparation experience is onerous, there is a greater temptation to discontinue the program. It's like starting a jogging regimen. If you go out and try to run six miles on the first day, you'll become stiff, sore and will drop out of the program. Doubling up defeats the program's intent, which is to learn something, not just to collect stickers redeemable toward a designation.

Tip #12: Explore Off-the-Shelf Study Aids

Don't rule out use of commercial study aids, though, despite the lack of official IIA sanction. One CPCU candidate failed the Accounting and Finance exam after taking a class, but later passed it after ordering a commercial package which included cassette tapes.

This is no advertisement for or endorsement of one preparation course over another, but you should be aware of what is available:

■ Insurance Achievement (800) 535-3042
7330 Highland Rd., Baton Rouge, LA 70808.

■ Jack C. Kier, Inc., P.O. Box 1183, Middletown, OH 45042, (800) 795-5347.

■ The Burnham System (800) GET-CPCU
253 Pleasant St., Southbridge, MA 01550.

■ Educational Training Systems (800) 225-9290
116 Middle Rd., Southborough, MA 01772.

■ The Merritt Company (800) 638-7597
P.O. Box 955, Santa Monica, CA 90406.

Other study aids include work books, pre-printed flash cards and books offering "canned" answers to past exams.

Tip #13: Become a Study "Flasher"

Create your own flash cards based on the questions and vocabulary terms in the Course Guides. Four-by-six-inch index cards are handy for this purpose. After reading a section of text, go back through it and the Course Guide and prepare flash cards based on that section. Pretty soon you'll have a handy and portable information bank to draw from once your study phase ends and your review/exam preparation stage begins. Flash cards become your own form of "software" which doesn't even require a computer. Success in exam preparation may very well be "in the cards."

Tip #14: Use Homemade Study Tapes

A frugal alternative is to compose your own study tapes on cassettes. For a fraction of what it costs to buy commercially available tapes, you can make your own. The tradeoff is the time — as opposed to money — you must spend creating your own. Solution: Dictate flash card materials onto blank cassettes. If you have a car cassette player or Walkman-type of machine, study and review while commuting to and from work, driving to appointments and while stuck in traffic. One Travelers executive studied for CPCU and CLU exams by listening to tapes while jogging!

> Ken Jenson, 28, a Los Angeles salesman, used to spend much of his hour-long commute singing to the radio. Last year he stopped the music and began studying to become a stockbroker. "I made tapes of the texts and took notes while I listened on the drive to and from work," explains Jenson, who is now a broker in the Westwood office of Merrill Lynch.[2]

Take a page from Ken Jenson's book (or tape) and view commuting time as a gift. Accept the traffic jam and the fact that you can't do anything about it, **except** to put that extra time to your good use.

Research on the learning process shows that retaining new material is increased dramatically by certain taping techniques. Take a new phrase or vocabulary term and repeat it on the tape in three different tones of voice. Play soft baroque music (by Bach, Handel or Vivaldi, for instance) in the background. Listening to these tapes has yielded huge gains in learning. (For more information about homemade tapes on any subject, see **Superlearning** by Ostrander.)

Tip #15: Cram Cramming!

Avoid cramming, or studying the night before an exam. If you don't know the material by then, you probably won't learn in on the eve of the exam. Last-minute studying often induces panic. Pace yourself so you don't have to face a crisis atmosphere just before the exam. See a movie, take a long walk, but clear your head and don't indulge in last-minute cramming.

Tip #16: Adopt a Sensible "Night Before" Ritual

Set out all materials the night before the exam: exam admission ticket, extra pens or pencils, calculator, watch, aspirin, etc. Scurrying around the morning of the test hunting for materials puts you in a bad frame of mind. Don't make the mistake of one CPCU candidate I know, who upon taking the CPCU Accounting Exam for the second time, realized right outside the exam center that she had forgotten her calculator!

Give yourself an immediate advantage over less-prepared candidates by arriving at the exam center with plenty of time (say, at least 30-45 minutes) to spare. Other time-saving rituals once you get inside the exam center:

- Read the exam booklet and complete the identification blanks.
- Number the pages in the exam book if you want to pace yourself.
- If you're through before the full time is up, use this time to: review your answers; make sure you've answered each sub part to each question; proofread your answers for spelling, punctuation, anything that will make things easier for the graders.
- Pray!

Tip #17: Forge Ahead

A week or two before the exam, order the books for the *next* course you plan to take. The momentum and sense of accomplishment you feel from completing one exam can carry over and lend impetus toward pushing onward or capitalizing on this feeling. You don't necessarily have to begin studying immediately after the exam. (That may be the last thing you feel like doing!) The new books will, however, serve as a tangible reminder of your mission: continued professional development.

Aiming For a Degree

Tip #18: Back To School?

Many entering the adjusting profession develop a longing to

acquire an additional degree, most often in law or business.

Maybe this is due in part to the daily dealings with attorneys, and the notion that "I can do better than that!" Maybe this impulse flows from the feeling that adjusters are the Rodney Dangerfields of the insurance profession who "get no respect," and that having the initials "J.D." or "M.B.A." after the name lends instant credibility. Still others may want a complete career change, and see claims work as a springboard to a career in law or other business fields. Those who juggle a full-time job with returning to school will have their time management abilities severely tested. Before doing this, though, engage in some introspection to see whether you are truly committed to this.

Does the modern claims professional need a law or graduate business degree? Claims professionals are expected to be experts in many fields: law, medicine, contract interpretation, coverage analysis, damage estimation, etc. While technical knowledge is critical, an often overlooked component for successful claims-handling and management is plain vanilla common sense. No graduate program (or any continuing education program, for that matter) teaches common sense.

Assuming one plans to stay in the insurance industry, the adjuster with a law or graduate business degree will probably have a "leg up" on others in terms of career advancement opportunities. This credential may be the adjuster's springboard to claims management, risk management or staff counsel. No one is certain, for instance, how many MBA's enter the insurance business, but one would venture to guess it is a low percentage. This is not to suggest, however, the insurance industry does not need such individuals.

Evening programs for business or law degrees are increasingly available, especially in large cities. Many of these programs cater to busy professionals, holding classes at night or on weekends. Executive MBA programs, for example, serve seasoned career individuals who are already well along in their careers. Often, all the classes are on weekends, in order to minimize the impact on the work day. Even so, this is a huge time commitment, both in terms of number of years as well as sacrificing personal time on evenings and weekends.

Most of the time management tips presented for CPCU/IIA preparation apply equally well to the adjuster who returns to school. Demands for intelligent time management will intensify for those involved with formal classes leading to a degree. Those charting this course should let their employer know of such plans in advance. This will serve many purposes:

(1) it prevents conflicts which might arise between the demands of class/study and work projects which can be completed only after hours;
(2) it may prompt a benevolent employer to adjust workload to accommodate the outside academic commitment;
(3) some financial tuition assistance may be available; and
(4) at minimum, it will let the employer know that you are working on professional development, and this may enhance chances for job advancement.

Tip #19: Keep Current on Trade Journals

Doctors worth their salt keep up with *The New England Journal of Medicine*. Any self-respecting attorney reads the *ABA Journal*. As professionals, claims people must similarly keep abreast of what is happening in their field, whether it be policy form changes, court decisions affecting claims-handling or what other companies are doing to streamline their operations.

Unfortunately, many claims people feel so overwhelmed by their workload they see such professional reading as a luxury. The trouble finding time extends up the management hierarchy, in all businesses. In one survey of 500 CEO's, 83% said they lacked time to keep up with reading in their own field.[3] Still, claim professionals must find ways to carve out time for keeping up with developments in their industry. Some of the more prominent publications with which any claims professional should be familiar include:

• *Claims*. Published monthly in Seattle, this magazine is targeted entirely to the claims profession. It includes regular columns on various aspects of claims handling, and offers a good overview of claim trends and losses throughout the country. The focus is on claims education and professional advancement. Publishes annual directories of claims associations and educational resources, as well as a monthly test question and answer from the AIC program.

- *National Underwriter.* This weekly, published in Cincinnati, is not aimed specifically at claim professionals, but rather at the entire insurance industry, especially the company and agent/broker sides of the business. Useful for tracking industry trends, and giving a broader perspective often lost when adjusters are up to their necks in files.
- *Business Insurance.* This weekly is targeted for risk management and employee benefit professionals, but do not be put off by that. Like the other weekly, *Business Insurance,* based in Chicago, follows industry trends and provides a glimpse of the "big picture." Unlike *National Underwriter,* it does not follow developments in personal lines insurance, however.
- *CPCU Journal.* Published quarterly from Malvern, Penn., each issue usually contains at least one article dealing with some aspect of claims. Recent samplings: "Status of the Seat Belt Defense, "Claims Investigations — Are They Going Our of Style?" and "In Search of the Excellent Claim File."
- Local Claims Association Publications. Usually these are published by state or regional claims associations, monthly or quarterly. Their strength is that they can focus on claim developments and practices within the adjuster's own jurisdiction, something beyond the scope of most national publications.
- *Best's Review* (Property/Casualty Edition). Though this monthly, published in Oldwick, N.J., is more geared to agents and underwriters, it sometimes contains instructive articles on policy interpretation, claims negotiation and industry trends.
- *Risk Management.* Published by the New York-based Risk and Insurance Management Society (RIMS) monthly. Though geared primarily to corporate risk managers, each issue usually contains instructive articles on coverage, law or some aspect of loss adjustment.
- *For the Defense.* Monthly magazine published by the Defense Research Institute of Chicago, a national group of defense lawyers. The target audience is defense attorneys, but they have articles which track legal developments which impact claim handling and defense.

Due to the number and variety of publications relevant to the claims and insurance industry, selectivity is essential. Some suggestions on how to keep up with the literature in your field without turning it into a full-time job:

Tip #20: Be Realistic in Reading Expectations

Don't sit down and read all the magazines cover to cover. Scan the table of contents quickly to see what articles would be of interest to you. Be selective. Don't ignore them, either, thinking "I'm too busy with my job and with my personal life to be reading about this stuff."

Tip #21: Use the "Rip and Read" Technique

Try this "rip and read" technique: When you see an article that you find interesting but don't have the time right then and there to read it, remove it from the periodical and put it in a separate "Reading" folder. Fill this folder and pack it when you travel and have a few spare minutes. A folder of articles is less daunting than a depressing stack of unread journals.

Tip #22: Scan First — Read Later

Later, go back and read those articles when you have the time. Practice the art of skimming, to quickly zero in on those topics of interest to you.

Tip #23: Schedule Regular Periods for Trade Journal Reading

Make time for this kind of reading. Keep a file in your briefcase. Use waiting time, lunch breaks and other "scraps of time" to keep abreast!

Tip #24: Learn to Speed-Read

Consider taking a speed reading course. Many are relatively inexpensive, and some offer free lifetime refresher courses.

Adjusters don't have to become "grinds" in order to stay aware of what is happening within their industry or company. All it takes is a little discipline and a wise budgeting of time.

Tip #25: Make the Most of Professional Associations

Most claims professionals belong to one or more job-related associations such as local or state claims associations, Order of the Blue Goose, Insurance Women, CPCU Chapter, etc. No one person could attend every meeting but, on the other hand, there is a need to stay involved. Meetings are a part membership in these organizations. Many of these meetings are held after work hours, so attendance may stretch what is already a long work day.

A few suggestions on how to get the most out of your memberships in professional associations:

Tip #26: Screen Topics in Advance

Screen ahead of time for topics of interest. If your specialty is commercial property losses, you probably won't be interested in a speaker holding forth on "Management of Carpal Tunnel Syndrome."

Check out the guest speaker and faculty or get an advance copy of the program. Will this person have anything of interest to say to you? Are they well-credentialed? Don't wait until you're already at the meeting to find out. Unless you're attending for social reasons, skip meetings featuring a topic or speaker foreign to your field.

Tip #27: Explore Taping

If the topic is one in which you are interested and your schedule keeps you from attending, check in advance to see if the meeting can be taped. If so, have a friend or co-worker tape it for you. Maybe you can even work out a reciprocal swap-off arrangement whereby you alternate attending and taping meetings. Later, at your leisure, listen to the tape and catch up on the meeting. Some sessions offers audiotapes and workbooks at a fraction of the cost of attending the seminar. Extract the benefits of the session without having to attend in person.

Tip #28: Mix Business with Pleasure

Rather than viewing the meetings with dread, view them as opportunities for learning:
- about clients;
- about changes in your field;
- about prospective clients;
- about your competition;
- about networking — swap business cards and build your Rolodex!

If you're working on a case involving another carrier, perhaps you can do a little business here. Be careful, though. Not everyone is in a business frame of mind or wants to do business at these meetings. Feel your way through here. Work the room!

Professional associations may be seen as a necessary evil, but their meetings can be viewed as serving a combined business and social function. Applying time management principles will make membership and meetings a more fruitful investment of energies.

Tip #29: Seminars and Symposia

Aside from association meetings, the claim professional's time is still consumed by continuing education seminars. Usually these are separate from claim association meetings. Topics of interest are presented not only by claims associations but by law firms, allied industries (e.g. construction, auto repair), rehabilitation firms, structured settlement companies. Your own company may host a seminar and require you to attend. Obviously, you cannot attend them all. Clearly you must attend some to keep abreast with what is happening in your field.

Such seminars and meetings, while essential, do not have to be a drag on one's time. Some suggestions on how to manage seminar and meeting time more wisely:

Tip #30: Attend Selectively

Don't be afraid to "just say no." Be selective in your attendance. Go only to those seminars bearing directly on your area of specialty or interest. Check the speaker's credentials. Advance material may clue you in on how well-run the seminar will be.

Tip #31: Combine With a Business Trip

Kill two birds with one stone! Combine seminar attendance with business in that same geographical area. Do you have any clients in that area on which you can call? Any prospects or business leads? Any investigations or casework that can be done in that area? Structure the trip so that it pays back in a number of different areas.

Tip #32: Order a Tape of the Seminar

Check to see if the seminar can be taped. Maybe you can persuade someone who is attending to tape the meeting for you, so you can listen to it at your leisure. Some companies may offer tapes (at a cost) of the session. Others may offer an audio-tape, a course guide or work book based on the seminar. Buying these materials may be a more efficient use of time than personal attendance.

Tip #33: Hold In-House Training Sessions

Consider holding seminars in-house. Many companies, physicians, attorneys and consultants are happy to visit your office to conduct an educational meeting. It's great marketing for them and an educational opportunity for you. All parties profit. One Baltimore claims office holds its own version of a weekly pizza party. Each Friday afternoon the manager orders in pizza and the invites a local defense attorney or professional to be a guest speaker on a selected topic for the claim staff. For visiting experts, it's a chance to market their services. For you, it is a chance to determine the length and content of the program, and totally eliminates time spent commuting to and from the seminar.

Tip #34: Require Debriefing of All Seminar Attendees

As a condition of allowing seminar attendance, require that the attendee return with a list of "take-aways" for the rest of the claim staff. Hold periodic office meetings and turn the floor over to the person who attended a recent seminar or training session. Give them ten minutes to expound on and distill what they learned at a seminar, whether it was "five ways to avoid bad faith" or "three tips on damage estimating." When the folks attending seminars realize they'll have to share their knowledge with others, it also helps keep their heads in the game while attending these sessions. It reinforces their own knowledge and disseminates these kernels of wisdom to those who did not attend. The trained becomes the trainer.

Whatever avenue of professional development you pursue, setting priorities is essential. This is a prerequisite for intelligent time management. What do you hope to accomplish? Associate in Claims? A CPCU designation? Law for the Claims person? Getting an MBA? Whatever it is, sit down today and write a timetable. Get with it! The bedrock foundation of being a professional involves doing a good job. That is a necessary but not sufficient condition for career advancement. Yes, there is (and should be) a life after work, and you need not sacrifice this to pursue professional development.

NOTES

1. Mattlin, *Sleep Less, Live More*, p. xvii.
2. "Trapped Behind the Wheel." *Time*, July 20, 1987, p. 64.
3. Myrna Lebov, *Practical Tools and Techniques for Managing Time*, Executive Enterprise Publications, New York, 1980, p. 1.

Chapter Nine

Avoiding Adjuster Burnout: Managing Your Own Career

"It's better to burn out, than it is to rust."
— Neil Young "Hey Hey, My My"
"The candle burning twice as bright burns half as long."
— Replicant designer in movie "Blade Runner"

Your stomach flutters as your boss invites you into his office and closes the door. You're the third claim supervisor who's gone one-on-one with the Big Cheese this afternoon. He invites you to sit down as he clears his throat and begins,

"Justin, your co-worker I. M. Pistophe has just submitted his resignation. Because management of this company believes in you, we are not replacing Pistophe, but are reassigning his files to your section of adjusters. This may increase their current caseloads by 20%.

"Since your relationships with key clients are so strong and we are under orders from corporate, I'm cutting your travel budget by half.

"Also, one of the draft clerks quit and we don't have approval to replace her. There may be some slight delays in getting payments out, but we're confident you and your staff can handle it.

"In addition, the Home Office has put its foot down about using moonlighting transcriptionists, so there may be a slight backlog from our harried in-house staff.

"Finally, Corporate is in a severe belt-tightening mode, and over the next quarter we need you to reduce your claim staff by a third. Who you opt to let go is your call.

"Oh, one more thing, did I mention the pay freeze?"

Part of managing your time wisely involves avoiding the peril of career or job burnout. You must manage not only the minute-to-minute and hour-to-hour time, but also take a big picture approach to managing the days, weeks, months and years which comprise the claim professional's career. As a vocation, claims adjusting is a demanding mistress. Like a jealous lover, the claims adjusting career can monopolize your time and attention, drive you to drink or divorce, and wreak havoc in our lives unless we find ways to manage stress. Adjusting has its own unique stresses and perils. In fact, Paul Leigh of San Jose State University has ranked claims adjusting as the 25th most hazardous white-collar profession.

No adjuster wants — or needs — to be on the wrong side of divorce, alcoholism or heart attack statistics. One way to do this is to recognize signs of burnout before they become pronounced and exact a heavy toll. On the theory that workaholics are burnout candidates, here is a diagnostic self-test to assess whether or not you are a workaholic.

Are you a "Claims Workaholic"?

The following questionnaire was adapted from one offered periodically by Workaholics Anonymous (P.O. Box 661501, Los Angeles, CA, 90066). If you answer "yes" to three or more questions, you may be a workaholic or on the road to becoming one:

_____ 1. Do you get more excited about your claims work than about your family or anything else?

_____ 2. Are there times when you can charge through your adjusting work and other times when you can't get anything done?

_____ 3. Do you take work with you to bed? On vacations? On weekends?

_____ 4. Is claims work the activity you like to do best and talk about most?

_____ 5. Do you work on claims more than 40 hours a week?

_____ 6. Do you turn your hobbies into money-making ventures?

_____ 7. Do you take complete responsibility for the outcome of your work efforts?

_____ 8. Have your family or friends given up expecting you on time?

_____ 9. Do you shoulder extra claims or work because you are worried that it otherwise won't get done?

_____ 10. Do you underestimate how long a project will take and then rush to complete it?

_____ 11. Do you think it is okay to work long hours on claims as long as you love what you're doing?

_____ 12. Do you get impatient with people who have other priorities besides work?

_____ 13. Are you afraid that if you don't work hard you will lose your job or be a failure?

_____ 14. Is the future a constant worry for you, even when things are going very well?

_____ 15. Do you do things — even play — energetically and competitively?

_____ 16. Do you get irritated when people interrupt your claims work to ask you to do something else?

_____ 17. Have your long work-hours hurt your family or relationship with others?

_____ 18. Do you think about your claims work while driving, falling asleep or while others are talking?

_____ 19. Do you work or read during meals?

_____ 20. Do you believe that more money will solve the other problems in your life?

The results of this little self-diagnostic quiz may give you insight as to how well you are managing the "big picture" time in your career. Failure to manage the big picture will pose certain career risks.

Adjusters are skilled at assessing risks elsewhere. To avoid burnout, though, claim professionals must be equally perceptive about their own careers, managing them in a way to maximize their energy. Here are twenty tips for keeping fresh and avoiding adjuster burnout. Adopting just a few of these tactics should help claim professionals handle the stresses comprising every adjuster's daily grind:

1. Watch the fuel gauge. Adjusters are the athletes of the insurance business. They must be quick and must have the stamina to work long hours and take enormous amounts of stress and verbal abuse. This is only possible if they eat as carefully as disciplined athletes. Think of food as fuel, not just filler. Consult Jane Brody's *Good Food Book* (Bantam Books, 1987). Remember the Russian proverb, "It's not the horse that draws the cart, but the oats." or perhaps, "It's not the adjuster who takes the statement, but the bran muffin." In other words, put away those Twinkies and re-evaluate your diet.

2. Exercise. Fueling your body is just the first step. Keeping the engine in good shape is key. In the gruelling and demanding work of adjusting, claims people who exercise have an edge over couch potatoes. Regular moderate exercise is sufficient. Twenty minutes of aerobic exercise three times a week is the suggested minimum. Try biking, jogging, walking, swimming or racquetball. Find an activity and establish an enjoyable regimen. Adopt the Nike approach: "Just do it!" You may soon find that you look forward to it rather than seeing it as drudgery. If you don't find time for exercise, you will eventually have to find time for illness. Exercise is an investment in one's health, not a selfish time-waster.

3. Take five. The body requires a minimum amount of rest, and the mind a minimum amount of dream time. Some adjusters need at least eight hours of nightly shut-eye. Others need less. Constant skimping on sleep wears you down, compromising the alertness that is so critical to adjusters' effective decision-making. Chronic sleepiness also makes one testy and irritable — qualities ill-suited to those dealing with the public daily.

4. Make time for family and friends. Adjusters spend most of their waking hours working. In the remaining hours, though, make time for family and friends, undistracted by professional concerns. Why marry and have kids if you never see your spouse or progeny? No adjusters have ever been quoted on their deathbeds as saying, "I only wish I had spent more time at the office handling files." The files will always be there. Your family may not.

5. Prepare "significant others" for upcoming demands. Inform family members in advance that you may be pre-occupied, if not incommunicado, during peak work times: an office move, a huge influx of claims from a new account or a natural disaster; a "crash" preparation period preceding a major audit; or any of the other 101 crises to which claim offices must respond. Adjusting work is stressful enough without burdening yourself with avoidable marital or family turmoil. Discuss these needs with your family beforehand so that your "support crew" will be there for you when you need them or can at least brace themselves psychologically for this stressful period, allowing them to weather it better.

6. Make time for yourself. That ancient adjuster Socrates said, "The unexamined life is not worth living." Time for yourself includes introspection, meditation, daydreaming — even self-indulgences. Go to a spa, read a trashy novel, vegetate under a beach umbrella, crawl in a hammock or soak in a hot-tub — whatever you find restful. As you relax, you will clarify what's important and enhance your enjoyment of life. It will also reduce the odds that you will begrudge the time you spend working.

7. Use all vacation time. Adjusters, perhaps more than average people, need time off to decompress from the stresses of their jobs. The point is to *take* vacation time. Don't skip vacations. Plan vacations that will be fun for you and your family.

Leave a phone number where your office can reach you, but only in an emergency. Phoning in every day is really a pseudo-vacation. Your mind as well as your body must be on vacation, or it is a pointless exercise. Leave office concerns behind. Return to your files feeling fresh and invigorated. Take time off after a major work project, like after pulling storm duty. Start planning your next vacation the day you return from your last one.

8. Spice up your routine. Work routine has pluses — predictability, reliability and consistency. Routine can also be mind-numbing, however. Avoid getting into a rut. Recharge by altering your routine occasionally. Change your time of arrival, departure or lunch. Vary your commute to work. Go somewhere different for lunch, with a different person. Breathe fresh life into your daily habits.

9. Expand your horizons. Remember life before becoming a claims professional? You probably had interests, hobbies and intellectual pursuits that have been dormant for years. Dust off that guitar, read a novel, go see a play, a funny movie, a concert, a basketball game — whatever you enjoy, as long as it's unrelated to insurance or claims adjusting.

Create oases for yourself which present opportunities for a breather: a picnic, a walk in the woods, or just doing nothing by lying in a hammock. This is healthy not only for you personally, but as a claims professional as well.

10. Plan a realistic work schedule. Avoid scheduling appointments too close together. Tackle priority and difficult work early in the day, when you are normally freshest. Allow ample time — extra time if possible — to complete tasks. Reasonable deadlines allow you to polish and refine. Pace yourself. Don't try to be SuperAdjuster.

11. Don't procrastinate. Inherent in the work of adjusters are annoying and anxiety-producing tasks — returning phone calls of difficult claimants or attorneys, taking a confrontational position, denying a claim, working on a burdensome file under a tight deadline, giving a client bad news, or travelling to take a statement in a rough part of town. Delay in facing these events only worsens the situation: your anxiety increases while the problem festers.

12. Get organized and focused. Your files, file cabinet, desk and work area should be tidy and well-organized. This makes you efficient and in control of your physical space. Being focused mentally is like being organized physically. Devote all your mental energies to one task at a time, rather than scattering them. (Laser beams are more powerful than flashlights.) When you have to do some thinking — an activity often hard in a busy, loud claims office — seek a place where you can work undisturbed — a conference room, library, or even your own office if you can arrange to close the door and hold your calls.

13. Be prepared. Use a diary or tickler system which tracks file deadlines and gives you ample notice well ahead of due dates. Anticipate and comply with client-imposed deadlines, and set your own timetables in the client's absence. When starting a new claim assignment, think it through carefully. Make a "to do" list for each file, and update it at each diary review.

14. Review all claim files regularly. At least every 30-90 days, review all your files to make sure that each one is progressing appropriately, and none has languished, especially the old "dog" which has already been handled by three preceding adjusters. You do not want to discover too late that the time for rendering a key report, responding to a demand or initiating a time-sensitive subrogation action has expired!

15. Call in help when needed. This takes many forms: brainstorming a file with other adjusters, assigning responsibility for different tasks among colleagues and support staff, arranging for other adjusters to cover for you when you are on vacation or on business travel. Make sure that allocation of tasks is understood so that nothing "falls through the cracks." Calling for help is not a sign of weakness. Being too proud to ask for it is.

16. Keep clients informed. Send clients prompt and regular reports and return all phone calls by day's end. Keep the client updated on the progress of an investigation, including positive and negative developments, and on settlement proposals. Ask yourself, "If I were the client, would I want to know this?" Do not wait for the client to phone about a claim status. Take the initiative. A well-informed client is a happier client. Happier clients tend to give you better business. A client should never ask a question which you haven't already anticipated and thought of first.

17. Nurture staff relationships. Adjusters are often only as effective as the people working with them — other adjusters, claim service reps, transcriptionists, secretaries, file clerks. Praise good performance promptly, in public if possible. Criticize inadequate performance constructively, and in private. Relate to members of your staff as people as you see them daily, not just on their birthdays or at the office Christmas party.

18. Plan. Do not wake up in the morning you are called to an accident scene only to discover that your camera has no film, your maps are at the office and you have only three sheets on your signed statement pad. Be prepared when duty calls.

19. Take your satisfaction "temperature" periodically. Evaluate your happiness as a claim professional. At least annually, assess what makes your work fulfilling and list obstacles to that fulfillment. Consider factors such as the types of claims you handle, your caseload volume, the people you work with, the quality and depth of your support staff, and your level of professional development compared with what you had originally expected to attain at this stage of your claims career. If you think making a few changes could promote your professional satisfaction, make them. Similarly, evaluate your stressors and try to reduce them.

20. Listen to — and heed — your body's signals. Be aware of the warning signals your body sends you when you are stressed — headache, fatigue, queasy stomach, neck pain. Ask yourself, "Why am I stressed now?" Change what you can to reduce your stress level. Your body will tell you if the change is working. Ideally, you will know you are over-stressed long before your body sends you these alarm signals.

A recent article on attorney workaholism contained some suggestions which are applicable to adjusters and claim professionals as well. Here are some of the tips:

- Leave 25% of your time unscheduled.
- Prioritize each task. Try to work on the most important ones each day.
- Break down big jobs into smaller chunks. Early in the day, finish something, even if it's only a small chunk.
- When you take on a new project or assignment, give up something else you were doing.
- Delegate more. When you delegate, ask your staff person, "Would you like to do this?" Avoid dumping only the unglamorous scut work on people, or pretty soon, they'll be less enthusiastic about having you delegate.
- Face up to your problem of workaholism. This is a big step toward solving it. Some people only get the message after a heart attack or divorce.

(Adapted from *Lawyers' Lives: Out of Control*, by Gerald Le Van, 1992)

These nostrums are better than chicken soup. They won't hurt, and they may help. Risk management has a personal, individualized component. Our profession poses unique challenges of stress, which produces its own physical and mental risks. Short of moving to the country and putting flowers in our hair, there are specific practical ways to avoid burnout and take a fresh look at each day's new challenges.

Chapter Ten

Managing New Technologies for Claims Productivity

Over the past eight years since publication of the first edition of "Time Management for Claim Professionals," many aspects of the adjuster's day-to-day work have stayed the same. Others have evolved. One area of change has been the proliferation of technology tools: e.g., desk-top computers, laptops, voice mail, e-mail, the Internet. These gadgets can be time-savers or time-wasters, depending on how they are deployed.

Let us look at how claim professionals can harness these technological tools for productivity and avoid time-sink pitfalls awaiting the unwary. Our discussion revolves around three major technology tools: e-mail, voice mail and the Internet.

Managing E-Mail for Maximum Productivity

Here are some practical tips for today's claim professional on using e-mail as a time-saver.

Tip #1: Check your e-mail daily. It does no good to have an e-mail address if you don't check incoming e-mail regularly. Log on every day at least once. Otherwise, you may quickly build a huge backlog. Further, there may be time-sensitive messages that are stale, simply because you didn't check your e-mail. Unlike the phone — which rings — or regular mail (a/k/a "snail mail") which has a tangible, three-dimensional quality to it, e-mail requires you to take the initiative.

Philosophers ask, "If a tree falls in the woods and no one is around, does it make a noise?"

Similarly, if an e-mail message is sent, but the adjuster doesn't regularly log on, does it have any value? Checking your e-mail daily also avoids the sinking feeling you get when you log on after a week hiatus and see, "You have 163 new messages." Ugh!!

Tip #2: Incentivize outside vendors to get on-line and to give you their electronic addresses. Encourage your outside vendors, especially defense attorneys, to get an e-mail address. Make it an item in the selection process. At my company, we want defense attorneys to be computer literate and totally comfortable in the electronic information age. Thus, we tell them that we consider a firm accessible by e-mail to be a definite plus.

Having outside counsel on e-mail can be very useful and time-efficient in communicating. For example, assume a client is fighting a claim and the plaintiff has disclosed an adverse expert witness, a Dr. Charlatan. The client phones, asking what you know — or can learn — about Dr. Charlatan. You consider posing this question to your outside defense attorneys. You can ask your secretary to compose 150 letters to outside counsel, asking them what they know about Dr. Charlatan. Alternatively, you can spend a week on the phone, trying to track down your attorneys. Or, you can take three minutes, compose an e-mail message, press the "Send" button, and disseminate messages to outside counsel. It should be clear which approach is the most time-efficient.

Tip #3: Build a directory or address book of frequently used e-mail addresses. For example, I have all client Internet addresses organized in one section of an e-mail address book. Defense attorneys that we use for product liability litigation are in another cluster. Insurance brokers with whom my company does business are in a third. These are organized so that if I want to send a "blanket" mailing, I can do so with a few keystrokes instead of selecting dozens of separate e-mail addresses.

If I want to tell outside lawyers that company billing guidelines have just changed with regard to what we will pay in photocopy charges, that is done in a few keystrokes. If I want to alert clients to a new study on electro-magnetic interference and its ramifications for their products, that is quickly done. If I want to offer insurance brokers a copy of our Claims Manual, I do not need to individually address each e-mail. The address book feature is a huge time-saver.

Tip #4: Circulate your e-mail address. Put your e-mail

address on your business card and business stationery. This lets people know another way to reach you. With this option, you reduce incoming phone calls and hard-copy mail. From this standpoint, e-mail is a tool to help claim professionals tame the telephone and manage paper.

Tip #5: Invest in e-mail manager software. These packages have many time-saving features, letting you:

- establish various address books of clients, attorneys, brokers, rehab firms, surveillance firms, etc.;
- compose outgoing messages "off line," saving money in metered on-line charges;
- download and read incoming e-mail messages off-line; and
- create various "file folders" for organizing your e-mail, based on topics that you establish.

Many e-mail manager software programs are available. If you access the Internet and send/receive e-mail through a commercial on-line service such as AOL, CompuServe or Prodigy, each may have its own product that you can purchase — usually at modest cost — to manage your e-mail and save time and frustration.

Tip #6: Use the "Re:" caption. Flag the topic in the "re" caption, just as you would in a written letter. If you don't, receivers see something a subject line that says "Internet Message" or "no subject." The receiver may think that it is Internet "spam," junk mail or something non-urgent, possibly deleting it or not giving it prompt attention.

DO NOT WRITE IN ALL CAPS AND UPPER CASE! If you write e-mail using all capital letters, beware. Your message may seem like YELLING to some readers. This is a tip from Nadine Udall Fischer, a communication consultant who is part of a growing number of people offering tips on how to deploy e-mail more intelligently. Some of her other ideas:

- Use e-mail for urgent matters only
- Be brief and complete
- Don't send anything by e-mail that you wouldn't want in the public domain

Tip #7: Realize that e-mail is discoverable. Want to waste time sitting in court? Include in your e-mail messages libelous statements about the claimant, policyholder or opposing counsel. Use e-mail to show that you engage in bad faith claim handling practices.

By contrast, if you want to stay out of court and boost your productivity, be careful what you put in e-mail.

E-mail is no more secure than a postcard sent through the mail. Courts have held that e-mail is "discoverable;" and don't think that your messages have vanished just because you hit the delete key. This is a two-for-one suggestion special: a way to better manage your time *and* your professional liability exposure!

Tip #8: Be selective in subscribing to mailing lists. E-mail mailing lists are terrific, but can become a time-wasting Frankenstein. The idea behind a mailing list is that you subscribe and then receive the postings of others as e-mail messages. The problem is that these can accumulate fast, and produce lots of wasted time scrolling through, seeking those messages which are relevant and interesting. "Spam" can clog up your mail box. This can cause your computer to stall while it downloads your 16 messages. Your e-mail "in box" can quickly hemorrhage with irrelevant and extraneous e-mail. "Unsubscribe" and disengage from any mailing list that has outlived its usefulness to you and that only clogs up your hard drive.

"Press '2' for Voice-Mail Tips …"

Let's look at some specific tips for claim professionals in using voice mail as a time management tool rather than time-sink:

When receiving voice-mail messages, incoming to your voice-mail machine …

Tip #1: State who you are. Do mention your name and department. Don't be so absorbed by your thoughts you forget to say your name, company and department.

Tip #2: State the date on your voice mail recording. This is a subtle way of showing callers that you're not simply using voice mail as a crutch for dodging difficult callers. If you say, "Hello, this is Janet. Today is Friday the 13th …" people know that your message is date-stamped and — presumably — you check your voice mail regularly. The onus is on you to make a new message each day. Otherwise, it is embarrassing to forget and on Friday have your message still say, "It's Wednesday the 28th …" This indicates you're not paying attention and does not make a positive impression.

Tip #3: State when you'll be available. Most callers assume you will respond in an hour or so. If that is unrealistic, indicate so on your message. You don't need to leave your life history. Are you out of the office? On a business trip? In a meeting? Indicate when you'll return or when you'll be available for calls.

Tip #4: Give callers a general idea of how soon they can expect a return call. Later today? Later this week? Next month? Calibrate the expectations of callers to minimize their irritation, impatience or disappointment.

If you pick up an urgent voice mail message that you can't attend to right away, then:

- forward it to someone else in your office to handle;
- ask someone else to call to acknowledge and to assure the other person that she will hear back from you by a certain number of hours or days; or
- make a quick call to the caller, indicating you're pressed for time right now, but just wanted to acknowledge his or her message and promise to get back to them with a more substantive answer by a certain time or date.

Tip #5: Coach callers on special features. Tell callers how to leave a message, especially if there are any unusual features. For example, may callers leave or send a fax by pressing a particular button or number sequence?

Also, how much time will they have to leave a message? Some voice mail systems allow a minute. Some allow an almost unlimited time. Others give you a warning when you are nearing the end of your allotted time. Others simply cut you off, maybe in mid-sentence. If callers are limited in time, let them know this. Can they replay their own message or re-record if they didn't like the first "take"?

If callers wish to speak to an operator and a real-live human being, state what button they should press for this. If you are having calls referred to a co-worker, so indicate.

Tip #6: Plan and instruct for emergencies. Explain whom to call for urgent matters. You may be out of the office working a fire investigation, traveling to see a client, or attending a home office meeting. Maybe you're on vacation. Perhaps you're out with the flu. Don't go into a family history on your voice mail message, but tell callers who they should contact for urgent matters. And urgent matters will arise.

Claim files — and claim urgencies — never take a day off. The files never get sick, have to attend a business conference or go on vacation. For the claims person, there is no such thing as a true vacation; there is — at best — just leave with pay.

Let callers know who to contact on urgent matters in your absence. This might be an emergency number where you can be reached. It could be a pager, a cellular phone or car-phone number. It might be your secretary or a colleague. Moral: make a contingency plan to stay in touch and accessible in case of emergencies. Manage your voice mail in a way to minimize frustration and maximize your productivity.

On messages that YOU leave on others' voice-mail machines …

Tip #7: Identify yourself. State clearly your name, phone number and company.

Tip #8: Spell it out. If your name is unusual, spell it. It is annoying when someone named Grzcwicwski calls and I can barely make out their name. When I call back, I'm in a guessing game, trying to approximate the correct name.

Tip #9: Repeat after me … It won't hurt to repeat your name and phone number, both at the beginning and end of the voice mail message.

Tip #10: Slow down! You're not in a speed talking contest. You don't have to sound like you're on Valium, but you get no Evelyn Wood Award for hurrying through your message at breakneck speed. This makes it hard for the receiver to jot down the correct name and phone number, increasing the odds of a mistake and miscommunications — a big time waster.

Have you ever received a voice mail message where the caller strolls leisurely through the first part of her message, then races through the phone number and name at breakneck speed? Don't subject callers to this type of frustrating treatment.

Tip #11: Leave your phone number! Don't forget the obvious: LEAVE YOUR PHONE NUMBER, complete with area code. Sure, the person you're phoning may have your number written down — somewhere — but why make them hunt it down? Business people find it irritating when they get voice mail messages from people who say "Call me," but who omit their number, like the receiver knows it by heart.

"Hi Kevin, this is Meg Smith calling on the Boeing matter. Please call me at your earliest convenience. Thanks." [click]

This kind of voice mail message, omitting the return phone number, is presumptuous. Now, I've got to locate the file and page through my Rolodex, researching Meg's phone number.

Tip #12: Remember the area code. Don't leave off the area code, unless you are placing a local call. It's always frustrating to have to look up the correct area code, especially when so many seem to be changing each day.

Tip #13: State claim- or policy-numbers. If you are calling another insurance company, leave not only your name and phone number, but the claim number or policy number. This helps the other party match up your call to the correct claim and expedite you getting a call-back.

Tip #14: Summarize. Leave a brief summary of why you are calling. This will help orient the other person as to the nature of your call and make your on-phone time more to-the-point and productive. Caution: don't get carried away. Make it brief. This helps listeners assess the urgency of your message, helping them effectively use their time.

Tip #15: Help your listener triage your message. Be helpful and considerate in leaving your voice mail message. If it is extremely urgent, indicate that. (Better still, with most voice-mail systems, you can dial zero to speak to an operator.) Have your target "paged" or find out who is pinch-hitting for them. If your call is not urgent, but somewhat time-sensitive, make that clear as well. If your call is neither urgent nor time-sensitive, so state on the recording.

Tip #16: Restate the question you're answering. If you are calling to answer an inquiry and get looped into voice mail, restate the question before answering. The person who left you the original message may not recall the inquiry they made. This avoids them having to call you back with the following message, "Thank you very much for your answer, but ... what was the question?"

Tip #17: Tantalize to induce call-backs. If you are calling to solicit interest — either to settle a claim or sell your claim services, hint about a special offer or a recent break in developments. This can tantalize the intended target to return your call.

Tip #18: Don't leave bad news on voice mail. If you have bad news to deliver, don't divulge it in a message; example: a problem on a claim, an unwelcome development, a huge reserve increase, a large jury hit.

Tip #19: Forewarn of lengthy messages. If your message is going to be long, forewarn the listener. Summarize the call's main thrust. Get to the point! If your message is detailed, ponder whether fax, e-mail, or regular mail is better suited for your communication.

Tip #20: Flag best call-back windows. When you call and leave a voice mail message, indicate when it is best to reach you. This keeps callers from wasting time. It short-circuits a variation of phone-tag, i.e. voice-mail tag: my voice mail talks to your voice mail, and when you call back, you get my voice mail, and ... well, you get the picture. When you leave a voice mail message, indicate that "The best time to reach me is between 8 a.m. and 10 a.m.," for example.

Tip #21: Say "never mind" if you later find the needed information. Call the other person back and tell them not to bother. For example, assume you cannot locate a claim number for a fire loss. You phone the agent or insurer to ask. You leave a voice mail message inquiring. Thirty minutes later, you pick up the claim number from a form that you had overlooked before. Pay the courtesy of phoning the agent or company back, telling them to disregard your earlier message. Otherwise, your future voice mail messages may get low priority.

The Internet as a Claims Productivity Tool

Hey adjusters — have you surfed the 'Net lately? Somehow, the image of a surfer is not the first one which comes to mind when thinking of claim professionals. Let's focus on the 1990s phenomenon of *Internet* surfing and how it can be a powerful claims productivity tool.

Whether or not cyberspace is the final frontier, it is certainly one of the newest. It is also one that claim professionals can harness as a time management and productivity tool. Armed with a modem and a computer, today's claim professional can reach out to other risk, insurance and claim professionals around the world.

Proliferating on-line services and computer bulletin boards have become bewildering. Cutting through the hype is difficult. On-line services can, however, be useful tools when deployed wisely by today's state-of-the-art claim professional.

Let's first examine some of the on-line services that claim professionals can explore as productivity and client servicing resources. In no particular order, these include:

CompuServe Information Service has a reputation of catering more to business clients.

Prodigy has bulletin boards which risk managers interested in claims might find useful, including an "Insurance" bulletin board under CAREERS as well as an insurance group on the "MONEY TALK" bulletin board.

America Online (AOL) is the fastest-growing on-line service, with bright, user-friendly graphics. AOL has an insurance bulletin board. The key phrase is "Your Money." Go to the bulletin board area, and under the bulletin board there is an insurance group.

RIMSNET is a product touted by the Risk and Insurance Management Society itself. You can capture RIMSNET daily news and can create a customized news-wire clipping service profile to get updates on specific topics of interest 24 hours a day, 365 days a year.

Recently-added RIMSNET features include a risk management database containing over 7,000 article summaries, and a "gateway" to a service called CDB Infotek. Through this, adjusters can access public records, such as nationwide motor vehicle information, civil and criminal court filings, business credit ratings, OSHA inspection reports, and other topics germane to claim professionals. Other services similar to this one are offered by commercial services on the 'Net.

RiskNet operates from the University of Texas at Austin and can be reached by the e-mail address risknet@risknet.com. You have to subscribe, but that is easily done and is free. Recent topics included using in-house versus outside legal counsel, the ramifications of discarding claim documentation and the discoverability of insurance policy limits.

Claimsmag.com is a service of *Claims* magazine, publisher of this book. On this World Wide Web site, accessed at http://www.claimsmag.com, recent articles from the magazine are offered, along with a library of related titles, links to many other sites and a moderated e-mail discussion area.

Almost weekly, it seems that someone new is offering an on-line service or Internet gateway access.

On the Internet itself are at least two INSURANCE "Usenet" discussion groups, like bulletin boards:

>   misc.industry. insurance (moderated)
>   alt.business.insurance (unmoderated)

On bulletin boards, adjusters can "lurk" or jump in and start posting messages and inquiries.

You can brainstorm about claim situations of common interest, pick up gossip, share observations and float trial balloons.

For example, recently I needed to locate firms providing temporary claim services. I posted a message on a major on-line "insurance" bulletin board. Within 48 hours, I had the names and phone numbers of two companies that provide adjuster temps. A few days later, a client called me asking about how to locate an insurance archaeologist, someone who specializes in locating old insurance policies for additional coverage. This can be *very* useful when you have a major claim and need to maximize your insurance. In response, I posted a bulletin board e-mail message and very soon had the name, address and phone number of a New York City firm called — what else? —"Insurance Archaeology"!

The Internet is a claims productivity resource in at least two areas: the first is Internet user groups and e-mail access; the other is the World Wide Web and web sites that can be a resource for anyone with an interest in claims.

Here are some of the uses of the Internet for claim professionals:

Tip #1: Brainstorm with other claim professionals. Often, it's easy for adjusters to feel isolated, as if no one else in the world understands their problems. In an age of rampant corporate cutbacks, downsized claim staffs are increasingly the norm. Forgive the modern claims professional if she feels like she's staffing a remote and isolated outpost, with few others within the organization who speak the same language, especially in the arcane world of claims. The Internet offers an antidote by providing a cyberspace equivalent of a professional support group, network and "kitchen cabinet."

Tip #2: Monitor specific industries and general business trends. Many on-line services generate daily news from Dow Jones wire services about companies in every sector of the economy. For example, my clients are medical device companies and biotech firms.

I use an on-line service to scan for today's news among all medical device companies and a separate search for all medical technology companies.

If I want to check FDA enforcement activities or see if any clients have announced recalls, I go to a separate area for FDA news. Total elapsed time: under 10 minutes. There is also a Dow Jones news retrieval service for insurance companies. Check earnings results, changes in management, etc.

Occasionally, you will find reports of litigation. Even if it does not directly involve you, it may be a harbinger of future trends.

Tip #3: Network and communicate with outside constituencies. The ability to send and receive e-mail on the Internet opens new ways to communicate with key outside constituencies, including:

- legal counsel
- adjusters
- TPAs
- actuaries
- other related services

In fact, some argue that e-mail has revived the once languishing art of letter-writing.

The phrase "caveat emptor" — buyer beware — or "caveat Internetter" — 'Net surfer beware — certainly applies to on-line communication. You can get plenty of on-line claims advice, but not all of it is sound. The input you get comes with no representations and warranties. You get what you pay for in the way of advice. Still, you have a chance to make contacts, swap ideas, network and use other claim professionals as sounding boards for your ideas.

The Internet's relative anonymity makes some people let their guard down and ask questions — or offer feedback — that they might be reluctant to do with their "game face" on during a more formal meeting. While there is an abundance of chat, opinions and information, some of it is sound and some is drivel. Claim professionals must sift the cyberspace wheat from the chaff, though that is a challenge not unique to on-line communications.

Tip #4: Neuter hostile expert witnesses. If you have an expert witness which has been noted against you, you can "network" with outside counsel to see if any of them know anything about him or her: prior trial testimony, deposition transcripts, credentials, weaknesses, biases, skeletons in the closet, etc.

Tip #5: Cultivate friendly expert witnesses. If you need a friendly witness on a particular point, one e-mail posting to your network of outside legal counsel may get more bang for the buck.

Tip #6: Build your own defense network. If you disseminate e-mail addresses among your legal counsel, you can foster a genuine network among them. They can communicate directly, compare notes, share information, share briefs, legal research, alert you to nascent trends, and so on. These activities often redound to the benefit of claim defense.

If you need an attorney in an area where you're *not* well-stocked, an e-mail message to your existing network may yield some promising referrals.

For instance, one large client — a $1 billion company — phoned me at 4:45 on Friday afternoon. It needed a defense attorney in India. Did I know of any? Truth is, I didn't. That night, though, I composed a message to my outside legal counsel and sent it via Internet e-mail. By Monday morning, I had a dozen leads for defense attorneys in India. The client, duly impressed, didn't know how I got them. To the client, who was thoroughly impressed though, I had delivered promptly. Moral: the Internet can be a time-saving claim service tool.

Tip #7: Disseminate service and billing standards. Quickly update your network of outside counsel regarding changes in your claims-handling procedures: billing updates, reporting procedures, etc. This saves lots of time and money.

Tip #8: Report losses promptly. You can arrange for the option of loss reporting via the Internet: from policyholders to the claims department, or from the claims department to outside legal counsel.

Adjusters also can deploy the Internet as a competitive edge in servicing. Let me offer one example. Brady Smith, Product Development Specialist at Mutual of Enumclaw, states, "The Internet can be a real asset in claims-handling.

"After a couple major windstorms in our area, power and telephone lines were down in outlying regions. Cellular phone circuits were overloaded. If you were lucky to find a working phone, calling a claims office got you a continuous busy signal. If you had a claim, you were out of luck until the line cleared.

"Many of these people did make it to the office and had PCs, though. An insurance company with a Web site claims form would have a leg-up on customer service in receiving a claim and communicating with its adjusters, making full use of the Internet's design specifications (communicating when normal communications are disrupted) to help the people needing assistance."

"Websession" is a time-management challenge for claim professionals who would harness the Internet as a productivity tool. No, Websession is not a new Calvin Klein fragrance. Rather, it is failing to recognize and monitor the "opportunity cost" from 'Net surfing; whiling away time on non-value-added surfing. Some people get addicted to 'Net surfing. Before you know it, minutes melt into hours as you stare hypnotically at a cool Web-site or go off on tangents far afield from your original interest. This can cause claims people to fritter away time that could be deployed more productively.

There is an opportunity cost in cruising the Internet. You're spending time with a computer that you could be spending on *people* and *projects*. The humorist Dave Barry likens the Internet to "CB radio ... with typing." The Internet is like a new toy to some people. Others can even get hooked or addicted to Internet surfing, to the extent that they become dysfunctional in their lives and jobs. Surf the 'Net, but only in moderation, so you won't have to enroll in a twelve-step self-help program for Net-aholics!

In fact, some doctors have identified the leading clinical signs of "Websession" ...

TOP FIVE SIGNS THAT YOU'RE "WEBSESSED"

5. You view your office gadgets as "friends" but forget to send your mother a birthday card.
4. You disdain people who use low baud rates.
3. You own a set of those itty-bitty screwdrivers and you actually know where they are.
2. You use the phrase "digital compression" without thinking how strange your mouth feels when you say it.

And the number one sign ...

1. Al Gore strikes you as an intriguing fellow.

As Peter Kent of Dover, Mass., stated in "Newsweek" magazine, after it published a lengthy piece by Bill Gates,

> Computers do provide good services, but the side-effect is a decrease in physical activity and a dependence on computers for both entertainment and companionship.
>
> — Newsweek, Dec. 18, 1995, p. 16, "Bill Explains it All to You"

Or, as one commentator wrote,

> The average American is too busy earning a living or getting a life to waste time perched in front of a monitor discussing the mood swings of lambs with Mongolian sheepherders or the sex life of the ring-tufted barn swallow with Norwegian bird-watchers.

In using the Internet, ask yourself periodically, "Is this time that *adds value* or productivity to my claims job, or am I doing the cyberspace equivalent of channel-surfing?"

Or ... "Am I becoming a cybernetic couch-potato?"

As an information resource for claim professionals, the Internet can be used or abused. If we're not careful, the Internet may go the way of television: once considered a key technological advance but now a source of mindless programming.

In answer to Microsoft's marketing question, "Where do you want to go today?", more and more adjusters should consider as one answer ...

Outside ... investigating claims!

Few adjusters have the luxury of whiling away the time in this manner, but going on-line is habit-forming. One must weigh the opportunity cost of "surfing," compared to other productive activities.

Is it time that could better be deployed to other purposes, such as catching up on reading back issues of *Claims* magazine? Or devoting time to working your caseload and settling files, moving claims, spending time with key people or projects?

Despite concerns over the 'Net's Dark Side of the Force, the anti-Internet Luddites won't prevail. The train has left the station. The only question is whether claim professionals will get on board. Computers and on-line services are claims productivity tools that are here to stay. The challenge is to harness the technology in ways which help us manage claims better and faster.

As author and motivational speaker Denis Waitley says, "In the years to come, you'll either be on-line or in a bread line."Maybe a bit of hyperbole, but it contains a kernel of truth for today's claim professional looking to turn time — the scarcest resource — into a competitive productivity and business advantage.

Technology tools can never replace the need for personal, palpable contact with clients, claimants, policyholders and co-workers. New technology offers new tools. Like any tool, they can be used or abused; deployed as time savers or time-wasters. Use these tips to harness new technological tools and to turbo-charge your professional claim productivity.

Chapter Eleven

Conclusion: Going For The Goal

The world's most powerful car engine is useless without a reliable navigation system on-board. Time management is a tool for claim professionals to use to achieve their goals. Time management and hard work are the rocket fuels to propel their careers. Discussing time management is thus incomplete without some attention to goal-setting. Results-oriented people tend to be more time-conscious. Similarly, efficiently managing time without thinking about your aims is like putting the proverbial cart before the horse.

Efficiency gets you nowhere without results. For what purpose are you making yourself more efficient? What do you hope to achieve with the time that you save? What do you as a claim professional hope to accomplish? As Lewis Carroll wrote in *Alice in Wonderland*, "If you don't know where you're going, then any old path will do."

Each claim professional should establish long-term, intermediate and short-term objectives. This gives you a target to aim for in managing your time. Since your efforts will be goal-directed, they will tend to be more motivated and efficient. Goal-setting has received much attention in management literature over the past ten years. Even if your company does not use something such as management by objectives (MBO), you should develop your own career plans. Manage yourself and your career as a one-person business.

Such targets can be classified by time-frame: short-term (one to six month planning horizon), intermediate (six months to a year or more) or long-term (over two years). Examples of short-term

goals might be:
- Top-producing adjuster for the month
- Finish IIA course in newt six months
- Close 30 files this month

Illustrations of intermediate benchmarks might be:
- Complete Associate in Claims program
- Promotion to next highest job category within eighteen months

Long-range targets might encompass:
- Promotion to claims manager
- Promotion to home office position
- Attain salary level to "X"
- Become an officer in the local claims association

Write your goals down. Don't underestimate the power that this has. The very act of committing your goals to paper directs your energies toward attaining them. It makes them more tangible. You are more likely to keep your eyes fixed on the target if your goals are written-down and available for quick review. Keep your ambitions private if you feel sheepish about them, but commit them to writing and review them at least weekly, preferably daily.

Psychologists often encourage people to use visualization to help them attain their goals. In your mind, imagine yourself as a claim manager or home office examiner (or CEO) already. Imagine your name with a professional designation beside it on your business card.

As you think, so shall you become.

As your subconscious absorbs these goals, your actions will be more efficiently directed toward attaining them, according to this school of thought.

Goals can also be categorized as to whether they are primarily process- or results-oriented. Being promoted to claims examiner can be viewed as a result. It is a milestone, not a final finish line but perhaps an interim checkpoint. Closing the highest number of cases per month or receiving two complimentary letters from clients each month are process targets which may bring the desired results closer to fruition.

Focus your energies in the right areas and your effectiveness multiplies. Also known as the "80/20 rule," the Pareto Principle in management suggests that roughly 80% of our efforts are spent on 20% of our problems. Twenty percent of one's business accounts for eighty percent of revenues. By focusing on the RIGHT twenty percent, one's effectiveness can be magnified.

As applied to claims management, the Pareto Principle suggests that:

- 80% of your time is spent on 20% of your caseload
- 80% of your phone calls are with the same 20% of the people with whom you deal
- 80% of your interruptions come from the same 20% of your sources

Moral: analyze and self-appraise your own time in light of the 80/20 rule. Try to find the critical 20%, whether it be in your "troublesome claims," staff absenteeism or client mix.

Without focusing on goals, time management for claim professionals becomes somewhat of a hollow exercise. Give some thought to your short-run, intermediate and long-term aims. Write them down. Relate your daily time management efforts to these specific targets.

So how will you use your extra thirty minutes or an hour per day? With better time management skills, the claim professional can get more done in less time. This is a very attractive option. By managing on-the-job time more productively, the claims person should have more free personal time available.

Effective time management involves acquiring new habits. Psychologists say it takes about thirty days to acquire a new habit.

Adjusters can take a buffet approach to the selections offered here, applying those which they particularly tasty and appealing. It is unlikely that one person could effectively incorporate all of these time management tips simultaneously. One suggestion, therefore: target a month, say, to work on managing paperwork. During those thirty days, practice the guidelines and tips offered in the chapter on "Fighting — and Winning — the Paper War." Another month, focus on "Taming the Telephone," and so on.

Reading about time management does no good and makes no sense unless you are willing to try out and practice the concepts discussed in this book. The adjuster must execute the ideas. In the context of time-saving habits, the adjuster must use it or lose it. Ultimately, the adjuster has the task of implementing these strategies.

Despite the unique time demands made on claim professionals, they have had very little to help them out. Many books, articles and bosses exhort the claims person to do more, without guiding them on how to do it.

A parable states that a turtle asked an owl how to get to the top of a tree. The own replied, "Sprout wings and fly!" The turtle responded, "That's crazy, I'm a turtle — not a bird." Undaunted, the owl retorted, "Sorry, I only set policy."

Well, doubtlessly the owl worked in the home office.

This is the unfortunate perspective of some who deride the calibre and skills of modern claims-handling.

Time is the claim professional's scarcest resource. They can lay claim to more time as their own, though, by applying well-established time management ideas in novel ways to their own work settings. This should make the adjuster's job easier and, dare I say it, even a bit more fun!

Let the end of this book mark a new beginning, a beginning in which you get your act together and become a more productive, efficient, effective and professional claim person. Experiment with new ways of doing the same task. How do you manage paperwork? Does the telephone control your waking hours? Do you feel like you're constantly spinning wheels on out-of-office time? Do you have difficulty finding the time and energy to get some badly-needed continuing education credential?

No single philosopher's stone exists for improving your time management skills. The secret is that ... there's really no One Best Way to manage your time. Any book or guru who promises you One Best Way is to be viewed with skepticism. You must be eclectic and willing to try and experiment with different techniques. Attack the problem systematically and on multiple fronts. Within thirty days you should see some positive, tangible results. So should your boss and co-workers!

Are you interested in learning more about time management and how it can give you a competitive advantage in your life and career? What follows is a list of other helpful books and resources on the topic of time management.

Well, we've talked about time management long enough. It's time to roll up our sleeves and put these concepts to work. I'd love to continue this discussion but, you see, I've got three phone calls coming in ...

Ready? Set? Go!

ANNOTATED BIBLIOGRAPHY

Thomas Are, **The Gospel for the Clockaholic**, Judson Press, 1985. A spiritual perspective for incessant clock-watchers.

Franklin Becker, **The Successful Office: How to Create a Workspace that's Right for You**, Addison-Wesley Publishing Company, Reading, PA, 1982. An excellent primer on how to set up your office or work surroundings for optimum efficiency and comfort. How to "make a statement" with your furnishings.

Kenneth Blanchard and Spencer Johnson, **The One-Minute Manager**, William Morrow and Company, Inc., New York, 1982. Time management is not the only goal behind this book, but the principles therein will save any insurance manager a lot of time.

Edwin Bliss, **Getting Things Done**, Scribner's, New York, 1976. A snack-food approach to time management advice. Each chapter is a one-to-three page snippet on some aspect of time management from A to Z.

Martin M. Broadwell and William F. Simpson, **The New Insurance Supervisor**, Addison-Wesley Publishing Company, Reading, MA, 1981.

William T. Carnes, **Effective Meetings for Busy People: Let's Decide It and Go Home**, McGraw Hill Book Company, New York, 1980. How to avoid time-wasting meetings.

Steven Covey with Roger and Rebecca Merrill, **First Things First: To Live, to Love, to Learn, to Leave a Legacy**, Simon & Schuster, 1994. How to prioritize what's important to you, from the author of **The Seven Habits of Highly Effective People**.

Merrill E. Douglass and Phillip H. Goodwin, **Successful Time Management for Hospital Administrators**, AMACOM, New York, 1980. Don't be fooled by the book's title. This book contains a lot of good advice for anyone in business trying to manage time wisely. Without knowing the title, you wouldn't guess from reading the book that its message was aimed exclusively at hospital administrators.

W. Ellis and W. Knaus, **Overcoming Procrastination**, New American Library, New York, 1977. A somewhat dry academic tome by two psychologists on dealing with procrastination. You could read it today or, on second thought, just wait until tomorrow.

Toby and Robbie Fanning, **Get It All Done and Still Be Human**, Ballantine Books, New York, 1979. Time management principles for the home and office. The authors argue that you can efficiently work your Fannings off and still be a real good person.

Charles Givens, **Super Self: Double Your Personal Effectiveness** Even if you don't care for Givens' investment schemes, this book is worth reading for the time-saving and time management tips contained inside.

B. Eugene Griessman, **Time Tactics of Very Successful People**, McGraw-Hill, 1994.

S.A. Hashmi, **Make Every Second Count**, National Underwriter Company, 1989. One of the few time management handbooks directed specifically at insurance professionals.

Dennis E. Hensley, **How to Manage Your Time**, Warner Press Inc., 1989. A Christian spin on the whole practice of time management.

Lauren Januz and Susan Jones, **Time Management for Executives**, Charles Scribner's Sons, New York, 1981.

Ray Josephs, **How to Gain an Extra Hour Every Day**, The Penguin Group, 1992. Over 500 tips on how to save time in your personal and professional life.

Alan Lakein, **How to Get Control of Your Time and Your Life**, Signet, New York, 1973.

Michael LeBoeuf, **Working Smart: How to Accomplish More in Half the Time**, Warner Communications, New York, 1979.

Myrna Lebov, **Practical Tools & Techniques for Managing Time**, Executive Enterprise Publications, New York, 1980.

Jay Conrad Levinson, **The Ninety-Minute Hour**, Dutton, New York, 1990. How to stretch sixty minutes into ninety by doing two things at once.

Marilyn Machlowitz, **Workaholics: Living with Them, Working with Them**, Addison-Wesley, Reading, MA, 1980. Punctures the myth that workaholics are unhappy and maladjusted.

R. Alec Mackenzie, **The Time Trap: How to Get More Done in Less Time**, AMACOM, New York, 1972. Lawyer Mackenzie takes an academic but very readable approach to time management. This writer's personal favorite. A new an expanded version was released in 1990.

R. Alec Mackenzie, **Time for Success: A Goal-Getter's Strategy**, McGraw-Hill Publishing Company, 1989. Beyond the to-do list: a way to help you meet your personal and professional goals.

Marc Mancini, **Time Management**, Business One Irwin/Mirror Press, Burr Ridge, IL, 1994. Very handy workbook. Practical focus. Part of Irwin's "Business Skills Express Series."

Everett Mattlin, **Sleep Less, Live More**, Ballantine Books, New York, 1979. Experiments on sleep deprivation and research. Thirty minutes earlier to rise and later to bed give you an extra work day each week. Not meant for insomniacs.

Jeffrey J. Mayer, **If You Haven't Got Time to Do it Right, When Will You Have Time to Do It Over?** Simon & Schuster, New York, 1990.

Jeffrey J. Mayer, **Winning the Fight Between You and Your Desk**, Harper Business, 1994. How to use your computer to get organized, become more productive and make more money.

Robert Moskowitz, **How to Organize Your Work and Your Life**, Doubleday & Company, New York, 1993.

William Oncken, **Managing Management Time**, Prentice-Hall, Englewood Cliffs, N.J., 1984. Examines the unique time management challenges of those in management.

M. Scott Peck, **The Road Less Travelled**, Simon and Schuster, New York, 1978. Not a book about time management per se, but wonderful insights about procrastination and self-discipline.

Frieda Porat, **Creative Procrastination**, Harper & Row Publishers, San Francisco, 1980. A redwood-tub California approach to time management, man, like wow. You know man, like you can be really mellow and still be into time management.

Arthur K. Robertson and William Proctor, **Work A Four-Hour Day**, William Morrow & Company, New York, 1994. How to achieve business efficiency on your own terms.

Sunny Schlenger and Roberta Roesch, **How to Be Organized in Spite of Yourself**, New American Library, New York, 1989.

Susan Silver, **Organized to be the Best**, Adams-Hall, Los Angeles, 1991.

Hyrum Smith, **The Ten Natural Laws of Successful Time and Life Management**, Warner Books, 1994. Time management secrets of the President of The Franklin Quest, a company which sells day planners and other organizational tools.

Jan Venolia, **Better Letters: A Handbook of Business and Personal Correspondence**, Tenspeed Press, Berkeley, 1981. An excellent guide to writing right, with a helpful section on the finer points of dictation.

Ross Webber, **Time and Management**, Van Nostrand Reinhold Company, New York, 1972. Very theoretical. Good if you want to know what Henri Bergson and other philosophers thought about the concept of time.

Stephen Young, **How to Manage Time and Set Priorities** (cassette tape), Network for Learning, New York, 1984.

George Walther, **Phone Power**, Berkey Books, 1986. Excellent tips on how to use the telephone to achieve maximum efficiency and effectiveness.

Stephanie Winston, **The Organized Executive: New Ways to Manage Time, Paper and People**, W. W. Norton & Company, New York, 1983.

AUDIO-TAPE SOURCES

Audio-Forum, 96 Broad St., Guilford, CT, 06437, (203) 453-9794.

Books on Tape, P.O. Box 7900, Newport Beach, CA, 92660, (800) 854-6758 or in California (800) 432-7646.

Conference Copy, Inc., 204 Avenue M, Brooklyn, NY, 11230. They specialize in taping professional meetings, conferences and seminars.

Dynamic Achievers Association, Inc., P.O. Box 144200, Coral Gables, FL, 33114, (305) 595-3321.

Institute for Human Development, P. O. Box 1616, Ojai, CA, 93023,

(800) 443-0100 X356. Self-improvement and subliminal tapes.

Insurance Achievement, 7330 Highland Rd., Baton Rouge, LA, 70808-6609, (800) 535-3042, in Louisiana (504) 766-9828. Workbooks, flash cards and cassette tapes for CPCU and selected IIA specialty designation programs.

Associated Management Institute, 1125 Missouri St., Fairfield, CA, 94533-6007.

Medi-Legal Audio Cassettes, 15301 Ventura Blvd. #300, Sherman Oaks, CA, 91403, (818) 995-7189. Cassette tapes focusing on medicine for law-related professions.

Nightingale-Conant Corporation, 7300 Lehigh Avenue, Chicago, IL, 60648, (800) 323-5552

Practising Law Institute, 810 Seventh Avenue, New York, NY, 10019, (212) 765-5700. Aside from a wide array of texts, PLI sells many cassette tape series on law/insurance-related topics.

Psychology Today Tapes, Dept. 729, Box 059073, Brooklyn, NY, 11205-9061. Adapted from the magazine of the same name. Tapes on self-improvement, enriching relationship, improving the workplace, etc.

Simon & Schuster Audio Publishing Division, Simon & Schuster Building, 1230 Avenue of the Americas, New York, NY, 10020.

Success Motivation Institute, P.O. Box 2506, Waco, TX, 76702-2506.

SyberVision, Fountain Square, 6066 Civic Terrace Ave., Newark, CA, 94560-3747, (800) 227-0600.

Waldentapes, P.O. Box 4142, Huntington Station, New York, NY, 11746.

Warner Audio Publishing, 599 Broadway, New York, NY, 10012.

About the Author

Kevin M. Quinley is Senior Vice President of Risk Services for MEDMARC Insurance Company and Hamilton Resources Corporation, Fairfax, Virginia. He has a BA from Wake Forest University and an MA from the College of William & Mary. He holds the Chartered Property & Casualty Underwriter (CPCU) designation and specialty (Associate) designations from the Insurance Institute of America in Risk Management (ARM), in Claims (AIC) and in Management (AIM).

A Contributing Editor to *Claims* magazine, Kevin co-authored the Insurance Institute of America's AIC 33 textbook on *Workers' Compensation Claims* and *Industrial Low Back Pain* published by the Michie Co. The author of over 270 published articles, his writings have appeared in *Business Insurance, National Underwriter, Risk Management, Best's Review, CPCU Journal, Insurance Settlement Journal* and *For the Defense.* He is also the author of *The Quality Plan: How to Keep Claims Clients Coming Back, Claims Management: How to Select, Manage and Save Money on Adjusting Services, Litigation Management* and *Winning Strategies for Negotiating Claims.* His sixth book, *Winning the Product Liability Game,* will be published in early 1997.

He teaches classes in insurance, claims and risk management for the Washington D.C. Chapter of the Society of CPCU, for which he served as President in 1992. A member of the Risk and Insurance Managers' Society (RIMS), he is a frequent writer and speaker on topics relating to risk-management and claims-handling. He lives with his wife and two sons in Fairfax, Virginia.

- Call **1-800-543-0874** to order and ask for operator BB
- Fax your order to **1-800-874-1916**
- Visit our website at **www.nuco.com** to see our complete line of products

---

PAYMENT INFORMATION

**Add shipping & handling charges to all orders as indicated. If your order exceeds total amount listed in chart, call 1-800-543-0874 for shipping & handling charge. Any order of 10 or more items or $250.00 and over will be billed for shipping by actual weight, plus a handling fee. Unconditional 30 day guarantee.

Shipping & Handling (Additional)

Order Total	Shipping & Handling
$20.00 to $39.99	$6.00
40.00 to 59.99	7.00
60.00 to 79.99	9.00
80.00 to 109.99	10.00
110.00 to 149.99	12.00
150.00 to 199.99	13.00
200.00 to 249.99	15.50

Any order of 10 or more items or $250.00 and over will be billed by actual weight, plus handling fee.

SALES TAX (Additional)
Sales tax is required for residents of the following states; CA, DC, FL, GA, IL, KY, NJ, NY, OH, PA, WA.

The
NATIONAL UNDERWRITER
Company

The National Underwriter Company
Customer Orders Department #2-BB
P.O. Box 14448/Cincinnati, OH 45250-9786

2-BB

_____ Copies of *Time Management for Claims Professionals:* ❏ (#347) $21.95

❏ Check enclosed*   Charge my: ❏ VISA/MC/AmEx (circle one)
* Make check payable to The National Underwriter Company
** Please include the appropriate shipping & handling charges and any applicable sales tax. (see charts above)

Card # _____ *Exp. Date* _____

Signature _____

Name _____ *Title* _____

Company _____

Street Address _____

City _____ *State* _____ *Zip* _____

Business Phone (___) _____ *Business Fax* (___) _____

e-mail _____

The
NATIONAL UNDERWRITER
Company

The National Underwriter Company
Customer Orders Department #2-BB
P.O. Box 14448/Cincinnati, OH 45250-9786

2-BB

_____ Copies of *Time Management for Claims Professionals:* ❏ (#347) $21.95

❏ Check enclosed*   Charge my: ❏ VISA/MC/AmEx (circle one)
* Make check payable to The National Underwriter Company
** Please include the appropriate shipping & handling charges and any applicable sales tax. (see charts above)

Card # _____ *Exp. Date* _____

Signature _____

Name _____ *Title* _____

Company _____

Street Address _____

City _____ *State* _____ *Zip* _____

Business Phone (___) _____ *Business Fax* (___) _____

e-mail _____

BUSINESS REPLY MAIL
FIRST CLASS MAIL   PERMIT NO. 68   CINCINNATI OH

POSTAGE WILL BE PAID BY ADDRESSEE

The National Underwriter Company
Orders Department #2-BB
P. O. Box 14448
Cincinnati, OH 45250-9786

NO POSTAGE
NECESSARY
IF MAILED
IN THE
UNITED STATES

BUSINESS REPLY MAIL
FIRST CLASS MAIL   PERMIT NO. 68   CINCINNATI OH

POSTAGE WILL BE PAID BY ADDRESSEE

The National Underwriter Company
Orders Department #2-BB
P. O. Box 14448
Cincinnati, OH 45250-9786